THE
POWER
TO
TRANSFORM

THE POWER TO TRANSFORM

90 DAYS TO A NEW YOU

CHRIS MAJER

with JOHN BRANT

RODALE

Mention of specific companies, organizations, or authorities in this book does not imply endorsement by the author or publisher, nor does mention of specific companies, organizations, or authorities imply that they endorse this book, its author, or the publisher.

Internet addresses and telephone numbers given in this book were accurate at the time it went to press.

© 2009 by Chris Majer

Rodale books may be purchased for business or promotional use or for special sales. For information, please write to:

Special Markets Department, Rodale Inc., 733 Third Avenue, New York, NY 10017

Printed in the United States of America

Rodale Inc. makes every effort to use acid-free ∞, recycled paper. ♻

Book design by Christopher Rhoads

Library of Congress Cataloging-in-Publication Data

Majer, Chris.
    The power to transform : 90 days to a new you / Chris Majer with John Brandt.
        p.   cm.
    Includes index.
    ISBN-13 978–1–59486–951–8 hardcover
    ISBN-10 1–59486–951–0 hardcover
    1. Strategic planning.   2. Corporate culture.
    3. Organizational change.   I. Brandt, John, 1951–.   II. Title.
    HD30.28.M324   2009
    650.1—dc22   2009009415

Distributed to the trade by Macmillan

2   4   6   8   10   9   7   5   3   1   hardcover

RODALE

LIVE YOUR WHOLE LIFE™

We inspire and enable people to improve their lives and the world around them

For more of our products visit rodalestore.com or call 800-848-4735

For Kendra—Whose patience and support got this all done. You are the one! For Cheyenne—This is what dad does and wishes for you. And finally, for Jac—You should have stuck around. You're missing all the fun and we are still missing you.

CONTENTS

INTRODUCTION

For most of your life, you have probably heard people talk about your potential—your untapped capacity to be, do, and have more than you are currently experiencing. Implicit in all of this talk is one of our core beliefs as Americans, which is that part of our birthright as human beings is our capacity to continuously reshape our lives. We are not forever bound by the circumstances of our birth or the occurrences of any particular moment and can, if we so choose and if we know how, reinvent ourselves and our futures.

The notion that there's more to life strikes a deep chord within almost all of us. We are drawn to the possibility. At the same time, we usually find some rationale for not venturing into this new realm: "I'm too busy." "I can't afford it." "Things aren't all that bad." "Now just isn't the right time." "None of that stuff works anyway." In the end, all of these excuses can be distilled into one word: fear.

You are afraid of being taken advantage of, afraid of what might unfold in the process, afraid of really changing, and most importantly, afraid that it won't work. You are afraid that you will expend time, energy, money, and emotion only to find out that you are one of those people who really didn't have any more potential after all. You would then be embarrassed and, worse, left with a life destined to be nothing more than a continuation of the present. For most people, fear trumps any deep-seated desire to strive for a different future.

This book speaks to the part of you that knows deep down that a life ruled by fear isn't much of a life. I am speaking to the part that knows you have somehow abandoned your dreams, incrementally compromised your standards and values, and have until now settled for a life that is considerably less than what you'd set your sights on and what you know is possible.

Deep inside, you know you have a vast, untapped reservoir of potential, but you don't know how to access it, so you settle for being busy instead of taking your real place in the world. That knowing yet unrealized you is the one that I want to bring onto the center stage of your life. If you are reading this and know that I am speaking to you—the you that knows something great is possible, the you that you really want to be—then you are ready to begin the process of transformation.

Transformation is a word that is often used but not deeply understood. Many people believe that it means an instantaneous change from one state to another; in other words, magic.

While it would be great if I could do that; a snap of the fingers and it's a whole new you! I am afraid I can't; I don't do magic. Instead I am offering you something much more challenging and profound. I want you to hold transformation as the process of fundamentally and permanently altering your way of being in the world. Transformation refers to a radical and revolutionary change in who you are and how you move through life. It stands in juxtaposition to the traditional methods of personal growth and development, which tend to be incremental and evolutionary. Instead, a transformational process allows you to make a dramatic amount of change in a little amount of time. The critical aspects that I am focused on are the nature, magnitude, pace, and permanence of change. I want you to set your sights on all of these elements as we move together to generate a new you and a new future for you. The fact that you are reading this book tells me that you are no longer willing to settle for incrementalism, that you have a commitment to something bigger with and for your life. It tells me that you are finally serious about stepping up and taking your authentic place in the world. Let me show you how!

To be clear the process of transformation isn't for the feint of heart. It will require you to look deeply and honestly at yourself. It will require that you be open to a completely different view of what and who you really are and what is possible for you. The journey will be intense, exciting, and, most importantly, rewarding in ways you can't yet imagine. That you are here with me now means you are ready, not just to change, but to transform!

This book isn't full of simplistic tips and techniques, sappy stories, or motivational pabulum. Instead, it lays out a simple, powerful process that has proven effective with world-class athletes, elite military units, real business leaders, top-tier companies, and tens of thousands of people just like you. None of these men, women, or organizations waste time on things that don't work, so you are in good company.

My promise to you is simple. If you do the work that is laid out in the book, within 90 days you will have completely transformed yourself and redesigned your future. I can't change you with a magic pill or the wave of a wand. But I do promise that if you follow the process as laid out in the pages that follow, you will have a new, more passionate, and satisfying life.

In exchange for my promise, you need to make one too. Your promise is to do the work, trust the process, and expect something extraordinary to happen!

ONE

THE HISTORY OF THE HUMAN POTENTIAL PROJECT

> THE GREATEST DISCOVERY OF MY GENERATION
> IS THAT HUMAN BEINGS CAN ALTER THEIR LIVES
> BY ALTERING THEIR ATTITUDES OF MIND.
> —WILLIAM JAMES

This is a book for and about you. It is for the you who watches in amazement as what you once thought to be solid and permanent institutions, businesses, and beliefs dissolve in front of your eyes, as you wonder if you have the capacity to cope with all of the change. It is for the you that asks if this is all there is to life, if you are somehow missing out on possibilities for something more meaningful. It is for all of you who have the desire to create a better life for yourselves and those that you care for and about. It is for the you that believes deep down inside that it must be possible to realize more of your human potential and use it to make a difference in the world. What you have in your hands is a handbook for an internal transformation: a rapid and substantial change in who you are, how you experience life, what you are capable of, and what you can accomplish.

This book will provide you with some insight into how you have become the you that you are. More importantly, it will open the possibility of both designing and delivering a new future for the you that you want to become: a new you. I intend to enable you to become that you, the you that you always wanted to be.

I have set out to lead you through a process that is meant to enable you to create a new and improved version of yourself: a more expanded, competent, and satisfied you. I know that right now you may not believe that it is possible to change who you are and have a future that is radically different from the one you are currently facing, but 25 years of experience tells me that it is possible. With that experience to back me up, I will believe it for you until you are ready to take over.

To realize more of your potential will require that you trust me to take you through the process detailed in the pages that follow. If you complete all of the work as set out, you can move through the process in 3 to 6 months. I know that as soon as you hear those charged words, "trust me," you probably start to get twitchy, most likely with good reason. Any number of speakers, writers, and would-be gurus make that same request. I'm sure many of you have spent valuable time and money in the pursuit of your potential, only to be disappointed. You found that change was nowhere near as easy as you had been led to believe, and this often-spoken-of potential of yours proved to be a bit elusive.

While authentic, lasting change may seem like the hardest thing in the world, that's because the current wisdom about how to make change happen is largely wrong. Before I tell you why I believe that, and why you can trust me to help you craft a new version of you and a new future for yourself, I want to start by introducing myself and explaining why I'm uniquely qualified to help you through this process.

With perfectly straight posture, his battle fatigues crisp and immaculate, and his fingers lightly laced together on the table in front of him, General John Woodmansee, a West Point graduate, Rhodes Scholar, decorated combat veteran, and commander of the Second Armored Division, United States Army, sat in a conference room in Fort Hood, Texas, waiting to hear how I could help transform his troops into stronger, faster, and more lethal soldiers.

Thirteen years earlier, with my hair down to my shoulders and my fist punching the air, I had marched down Seattle's freeways, participating in and eventually leading student protests against the Vietnam War while I was at the University of Washington. I had arrived on campus as a freshman in the fall of 1969, and by the spring of 1970 everything, including me, had changed. I participated fully in what seemed to be a new golden era. I played rugby, experimented with the exotic offerings of the day (yes, I even inhaled), and was social chairman of the Sigma Alpha Epsilon house. At the same time, I earned my "student radical" moniker and, like many of my peers, set my sights on changing the world.

I had been protesting the Vietnam War while Woodmansee fought it. Now, in the spring of 1983, I found myself standing in front of the general and his staff, hoping to do business with them.

As head of a Seattle-based company then called SportsMind (the original incarnation of the Human Potential Project), I, along with my team, had used a collection of practices we bundled together as Mental Fitness to show athletes how they could make their games and their lives more satisfying, meaningful, and triumphant. We combined our work on mental fitness with contemporary physical-training methodologies, and, in conjunction with work on developing passion, belief systems, and values, we offered a new and potent mind-body-spirit approach to sports performance. Our success with athletes had earned us a shot at convincing the leaders at Fort Hood to adapt our comprehensive approach for their troops. I knew we could help the Army. I just had to convince them.

The base's current physical training program was a relic from World War II and had proven woefully inadequate for the demands of the late 20th century. The troops were trained and tested on a set of exercises unrelated to situations they would face in combat and were evaluated by fixed scores. Failing to hit a benchmark filled a soldier with anxiety, as it singled him or her out for remedial work. Despite the exceedingly modest standards of the physical training test, a shocking number did fail, which resulted in our invitation to Fort Hood. Once there, we learned that the Army faced a host of other issues as well: generally low morale, too many overweight soldiers, too many sick calls, and rising levels of alcohol and substance abuse.

While soldiers lacked a sense of purpose and confidence, officers were being sent to business school to learn how to be managers. Still suffering an emotional hangover from the Vietnam War, the Army had lost touch with some of its vital history, and in its rush to learn how to manage, had forgotten how to lead. To its credit, the Army was clear that things needed to change and was willing to try our methods to solve its problems. We proposed techniques for enhancing spirit, passion, and teamwork along with our innovative process of building physical and mental fitness. We were, in short, using contemporary methods to reconnect the Army with its own core values.

"Your biggest dilemma is that you've been operating as if all your problems are separate and unrelated," I told Woodmansee at the briefing. "You're taking the business-school approach and putting poor physical-training scores in one box, low morale in another box, too many sick calls in a separate box, and drug and alcohol abuse in still another. You then have a remedial program designed to attend to each of the boxes. That burns a lot of time and money. You are pulling all of the threads apart, forgetting that they are part of the same cloth."

The notion that physical fitness could be "achieved" via exercises and techniques, for example, was a false, self-defeating premise. Fitness, I explained, was a process rather than a product; a way of life, not an achievement. The physical, mental, and spiritual development of each soldier and each unit were intertwined, contributing to morale, cohesiveness, and mission performance.

"Because all of your issues are related," I continued, "they can't be resolved with a series of narrowly focused remedial programs. We propose to help you solve all your problems at once."

This was a bold statement, and it caught the attention of everyone in the room. However, in order for General Woodmansee to accept it, he would have to believe in me and my team. We needed to present ourselves as living, breathing examples of the qualities we extolled. We had to model the states of being focused and centered, as well as to demonstrate the power of clear, accountable communication. Again, I was confident. I had embodied these practices in my own life, through my experiences with the Japanese martial art of aikido, in first-division rugby competition, and also in my business career. I believed 100 percent in what I was saying and doing, and I had equal faith in my teammates. I had special confidence in our next presenter, Horst Abraham.

Horst was a native of Austria. A small boy during World War II, he'd been sent to a Nazi concentration camp. At war's end, the camp was liberated by the Americans and turned over to the Soviets, who promptly imprisoned Horst again. Eventually he was freed and years later made his way to the United States, where he'd distinguished himself as a scholar and ski coach. He had published two influential books on skiing and served as a developer of coaches for the U.S. ski team. The eldest member of our team at Fort Hood (I was the youngest), Horst was an expert on fitness, peak performance, and nutrition. Tall, with a distinguished appearance and a courtly, old-world bearing, Horst Abraham was the kind of man who would impress General Woodmansee.

As I was preparing to turn things over to Horst for his portion of the briefing, however, I noticed that something wasn't quite right. Horst failed to radiate his usual grace and confidence. He looked pale and wouldn't make eye contact with General Woodmansee or the other officers. Instead of filling the room with his cultured, resonant, Austrian-accented voice, all he could do was stand rigid and drawn, barely moving and not saying a word.

We later learned what had happened: Confronted for the first time since the war with a roomful of men in military uniforms, Horst had suffered a paralyzing flashback to his searing experiences as a boy. My team and I were trying to convince Woodmansee that we could help his troops effectively perform in life-and-death situations, and now, during a routine briefing, one of our key people had turned to stone.

In a life liberally if not intentionally seasoned with more than my share of "oh shit" moments, this one loomed large. It was hot in Texas, and despite the air conditioning in the briefing room, I could feel sweat beading at the small of my back and my breathing becoming fast and shallow. My sympathetic nervous system was kicking in with the stress response. From years of both learning and teaching the practice of centering, which means being fully present in the moment, powerfully relaxed, and connected mind to body and self to the world, I realized that, at that moment, I was way off-center. Luckily, I also knew what to do to bring myself back.

Instead of trying to stifle my anxiety, which would only have made the situation worse, I took a deep breath. On the inhalation I relaxed the tension in my shoulders and neck, and let it go with the exhalation. I brought my attention back to my physical center—the point that lies roughly one hand's span below the navel and equidistant between the front and back of the body. Coming back to center generated a subtle but profound shift in my perspective.

The situation remained unsettled, of course, but I was now free from the grip of anxiety and able to act with focus and clarity. Okay, I thought: Horst has frozen. Seemingly certain success now teetered on the brink of an embarrassing failure. But I could still make powerful choices and maintain the dignity and identity of our team.

"Excuse me, sir," I said to the general. "Is it okay if we take a quick break before we move on to the next section?"

He agreed. The officers stepped outside for some air while my team urgently huddled. Horst was quick to apologize for what was happening, and when the rest of us understood what he was experiencing, we realized that blaming him would be cruel and futile. I mention this not to advertise our virtue, but to point out that, like centering, accountability, avoiding the impulse to blame others for our problems, is a valuable skill, one requiring practice, but which yields great dividends.

We decided that I'd pinch-hit for Horst. I was generally familiar with his material but was hardly an expert. I had never practiced, let alone delivered, this section of the briefing.

The officers filed back into the room. Muttering a quick prayer that no one would pin me down with detailed questions, I took another deep breath, looked to my teammates for reassurance, and then let it roll.

The next few minutes unfolded with a natural rhythm and fluidity; no one could have guessed that I'd never delivered this material before. Even I was a bit taken back by the power that was unlocked by honoring this moment's possibility, rather than cowering before its threat. My "oh shit" moment had been transformed into an opportunity to realize more of my human potential. When I finished speaking, the general turned to his staff, nodding in approval. He was impressed enough that he offered us a contract with the Army. We were assigned a test unit and deployed to Fort Hood. Before our pilot program concluded, the commander of a neighboring brigade, the famous Tiger Brigade, General George Patton's old unit, demanded to be next in line for our services.

At that point, without letting us know, the Army decided to test our program against its internally designed Master Fitness Trainer program, which it had taken 6 years to develop. The test was conducted using three different units, each consisting of roughly 1,500 troops. One brigade received the standard, World War II–vintage training, another underwent the Master Fitness Trainer regimen, and the Tiger Brigade followed our Combat Fitness program.

They tested the three brigades both before our program started and again 6 months after we completed it. Results showed no change in the fitness level of the control group. More surprising (and to the chagrin of the program's designers), the brigade using the Master Fitness Trainer program also showed no change. The Tiger Brigade, by contrast, which deployed our program, showed a 66 percent reduction in overweight troops, a 50 percent reduction in sick calls, a 60 percent reduction in drug and alcohol abuse, and a 25-point average increase in physical-training test scores. In a front-page story announcing the results in the *Army Times*, Tiger Brigade commanders also reported a dramatic increase in troop morale.

This success opened new doors for us, as Colonel William Potter, the Commander of the Tenth Special Forces Group, had read the *Army Times* article that featured our results and called asking what we could do with his operators. After a series of conversations, briefings, and negotiations (which took so long that by the time they were complete Colonel Potter had moved up and Colonel Jim Zachary had taken command), we ended up with a yearlong classified project with the Tenth SFG in which we had a blank check to push the boundaries of human performance. Two "A" teams came under our direct authority for 6 months, and in the process outperformed any others in Special Forces history in a series of mission simulations. This work in turn provided us with the opportunity to do a quiet project with the Navy SEALs and, years later, a project with the Marines.

At the completion of our work with the Army, we decided to branch out into the business world. In many ways, this new arena was more challenging. In business there are no time-outs, no off-seasons, no stand-downs. By our standards, there is no real training in business, and on any given "team" there is a vast gap in the level of competence and commitment on the part of the players. We were excited to see if we could make our mark in this new world, and indeed we could and did.

Over the last two decades, our roster of clients at what is now the Human Potential Project (HP2) has included Intel, Microsoft, EDS, Capital One, AT&T, Amgen, and Allianz. These firms haven't grown into industry giants by buying motivational pap or packages of useless tips and techniques. Like the U.S. Army and other branches of the military, these organizations entrusted their key players to us because they recognized the need to master the art of change. They understood that the tired methods of the past weren't going to lead them into the kind of future that they envisioned.

Among our scores of successful projects, we delivered what came to be known as Project Miracles to the Consumer Products Division of AT&T. The net effect was that the division went from breakeven to generating more than $3 billion in profit to AT&T over the course of 48 months. We helped Scripps Memorial Hospital, in Encinitas, California, boost staff morale, increase patient satisfaction by 40 percent, and win the Excellence in Management Award from the *San Diego Business Journal*, all within the space of 9 months. At Capital One we were entrusted with the development of five business units and 1,500 senior managers over the course of 4 years. Columbia House gave us its entire management team for 9 months, and in the process we showed the company how to stand up a new business unit in 7 months. Its previous best had been 18. That was one of 10 projects we worked on with the Columbia House team, and the economic value that we generated with that single project paid for our engagement.

So what did we teach these CEOs, executives, leaders, managers, and team members? An entirely new set of practices for leading, managing, and organizing a business; new ways to generate customer satisfaction, innovation, competitive advantage, and profitability. In short, we provided them with a comprehensive, coherent method for designing and delivering a new version of themselves, their organizations, and a new future for their businesses. Our corporate work is a combination of somatic (unified mind and body) practices, structured linguistic moves, performance principles, practices for managing moods and emotions, and supporting processes for designing and running the systems and processes in an organization. We refer to this body of work in its entirety as commitment-based management.

Not all of that will be of interest to you, but this should be: Fundamental to everything we do is the notion that what we hold as the absolute limitations of the world are merely the limitations of our own minds. What we think is a real impossibility is usually something we have simply made up and chosen not to question.

As I have progressed in my life, career, and my own learning, I have continued to expand my view on what it takes to produce transformational change. At the University of Washington I earned a master's degree in public administration with a specialty in organizational development. Through playing rugby for 10 years, I learned what it takes to build and sustain a real team. I got my original inspiration to step into this new world of human potential from the philosopher, journalist, and aikido master George Leonard. Over the years, I myself studied aikido with Hirata Sensei, spent some time at Esalen, and learned from teachers ranging from Zen masters to Tibetan monks.

By the late 1980s, I had put together a solid body of work that touched on the elements of mind, body, spirit, and team building. It was working well, but I had the sense that something was still missing. I was then introduced to Dr. Fernando Flores and his work on the idea that human beings live in narratives, that the interconnection of body, language, and emotion generates what we call reality. I came to see that there was a vast world of possibility that we had been missing. Turning this notion into a coherent methodology was not so simple, but I had the pieces.

As you can see, I'm a teacher who integrates a diverse set of traditions and practices into a unified whole. I have built a world-class team and been blessed with great students. And I'm convinced that the time for this material has come. This brings me to my reasons for writing this book.

Like most businesspeople, I have always worked with targeted audiences and segmented markets: first athletes, then the military, and finally corporations. At the conclusion of every training cycle, some of the participants invariably tell me, "I committed to this work hoping to become a better volleyball player (or squadron leader, or regional sales manager), but I came out as a better person." Then they want to know what courses I have that they can send their husbands, wives, siblings, or children to.

While gratifying, these comments also keep me awake at night. I have heard them often enough, from a wide-enough variety of people, to realize that everyone has the desire to lead the most meaningful and productive life that he or she can. And each deserves access to this material, because it works.

I started to tell you that authentic, lasting change is possible, and here is how I know that this is true.

I was born and raised in Spokane, Washington, which, in the 1950s and '60s, was still a quiet, conventional, rather uninspiring town, a far cry from the dynamic, sophisticated city that it has finally set its sights on becoming. Back then, mine was a *Leave-It-to-Beaver* existence. My father had taken over his father's Ford dealership and was chairman of the local draft board. I spent my summers at the local lakes and learned to ski at Mount Spokane. At Lewis and Clark High School I played a bit of football, served as president of my senior class, played in a rock band, and squired our Lilac Princess to the senior prom. In short, I was living the all-American story.

Then, in the fall of 1969, at age 18, I went away to my freshman year of college at the University of Washington, in Seattle. Eight months later, I was marching down freeways, taking over the campus radio station, and deeply involved in turning my past upside down.

I had grown up in one world and been thrown into another. Pervasive change and roiling ferment defined my coming of age. Often, during those electric years of the late '60s and early '70s, I felt like the ground was literally shifting under my feet. Everybody in America was sensing the same upheaval. Some people were threatened by the changes, others were frightened or enraged, and still others, like me, were exhilarated. The times instilled in me a deep and abiding sense that anything was possible, that humans possessed, by birthright, the capacity to develop lives bounded only by their imaginations, and that the United States was the one place on Earth where that was possible.

Forty years later, we live in a radically different public landscape. And yet, despite the dark, defeatist stories that we tell ourselves and hear through our media and popular culture, I still believe in the possibility and power of change. Thus it is immensely frustrating to watch as the vast majority of people sleepwalk through their time on this planet, arriving at death safely but having never really lived along the way. They have no inkling that everything they are experiencing is wholly and completely their own creation. All of the petty resentments, anger, frustration, and disappointments. All of the missing joy, passion, love, and connection. All of the unrealized dreams, broken relationships, and walled-off hearts. All of the dysfunctional families, financial failings, and dead-end jobs. You created it all, and you can re-create it any way you choose.

I'm not saying that the adversities in your life don't exist. To you, they do. Just consider the possibility that they aren't real, that they aren't solid and unchangeable. Every day we are awash in evidence that what we hold as "true, real, permanent, and impossible" is open to change. If you pay attention to something other than the mainstream media, you can learn about everyday people who overcome seemingly impossible odds to create a better life for themselves and others. People who have faced down daunting bureaucratic institutions, made their way out of gangs and ghettos, stood tall while others were cowed by injustice, accomplished some athletic feat that was said to be impossible, beaten fatal diseases, or found a way to bring heart and compassion to those people and places in desperate need of both. For every disaster and crime reported on the news, there are thousands of seeming miracles, good deeds, and people from whom we could take inspiration if their stories made it to the airwaves.

In my own life I have witnessed extraordinary acts of courage and selflessness, and met many people I regard as heroes and role models. This is the news that I choose to pay attention to. These are the stories I listen to.

I believe—I know—that the early years of the 21st century are every bit as electric and hopeful as the era of the late '60s. I've spent the last quarter-century helping individuals and organizations embrace and ride the waves of change. I instruct people in the craft of living the life they have chosen rather than the one they've been dealt. This means learning the practical but transformational skills of thinking clearly, listening deeply, speaking powerfully, and acting purposefully. Through practice, you can master these fundamental skills in the same way that you've learned to ride a bicycle or drive a car, in the way that an experienced carpenter cuts a 2-by-4 or a concert violinist draws her bow. You will learn to do them intuitively and instinctively.

You can quiet the chatter corroding your mind. You can experience less anxiety. Much of your anger and frustration can drain away. You can know less fear and guilt, grow less likely to blame or envy others, and achieve a liberating sense of control. Instead of punishing yourself for your perceived "failures," you can simply set your sights on a different outcome and work to produce what you intend. And because nature abhors a vacuum, the hole left by your anxiety, fear, anger, and guilt can be filled by confidence, clarity, passion, and ambition.

In the 21st century, economic, political, and cultural power will not go to the wealthiest nations or the ones with the strongest armed forces, but to an international collective of individuals who believe in and work toward the development of their inherent human potential. These individuals will be the most prosperous workers, the most effective leaders, the most creative artists and scientists, and the most fulfilled and responsible members of their families and communities. They will approach life as a challenging, exhilarating adventure. This book represents a distillation of what I have learned about earning membership in this global collective.

As we get deeper into working together, you will come to see all of this much more clearly. For now I am simply going to ask that you hold the possibility that with the experience I bring to the project of realizing your human potential, something extraordinary will take place.

In my own moments of doubt (yes, I still have them), I take strength from the memory of that briefing at Fort Hood. I can still see the skepticism in General Woodmansee's eyes turn to trust as he considered our proposal, looked at his officers, turned back to us, and said, "Let's do it!"

TWO

HOW TO USE THIS BOOK

> **MAKE NO SMALL PLANS FOR THEY HAVE NOT THE POWER TO STIR MEN'S BLOOD.**
> **—MACHIAVELLI**

At the start of every corporate engagement for the Human Potential Project, each group is split into three equally sized subsets. We refer to them as learners, skeptics, and prisoners. The learners are the ones who are excited that their company is being proactive and willing to invest in them. The skeptics are cautious about the possibility of change, willing to suspend judgment for a while but not for too long as they wait to see what we can do. The prisoners, finally, are the cynics. They sit with their arms crossed, all having taken seats in the back rows, convinced that we're wasting their time.

Cynicism is what we refer to as the coward's mood. These people trusted something or someone once, were let down or betrayed, and won't let themselves be burned again. Their mockery and hostility are nearly palpable. I love the prisoners; it never takes more than a few days to convert about 90 percent of them into learners, and then they become our strongest advocates.

I understand their resistance. Like most professionals, they have been subject to a host of so-called motivational programs, listened to lots of flowery language about the need for change, and know that none of it works. Despite the catchy slogans and the nifty shirts, mugs, and binders, things stay the same. They don't feel any better afterward, productivity doesn't improve, there is no new wave of innovation, and people fall deeper into resignation. When we show up, the natural reaction is, "Oh great, here we go again." I understand their feeling of unease. After all, my team and I are professional catalysts, which means that we are paid to produce a certain degree of discomfort, to unsettle them. Our art lies in being able to unsettle them in such a way as to convert their cynicism into interest and engagement.

The dilemma that they, you, and we face is simple. There is no learning inside your comfort zone. Until you put yourself on the line, move out of your comfort zone, and take a chance, you will never achieve any real progress. Over time, this adventurous state of mind can become your new standard, replacing your fear, complacency, self-doubt, and resistance.

For you, the reader, my presence poses both an opportunity and a threat. Some deep part of you is yearning for more: to learn, expand, grow, experience more of yourself and life. At the same time, your mind is threatened, as it is deeply committed to playing it safe, being right, and looking good. Change is a threat to your current state of being, and no matter how much you agree with the concept or see the need for change, your mind is invested in the status quo.

As you work through this book, you're going to learn a brand-new set of practices. These new practices will allow you to develop what we call *embodied competence*. That means you will be able to take the new actions without having to stop and think about them, or even refer back to this book. These new practices will become embodied—literally part of you—in the same manner that riding a bicycle and tying your shoes are embodied practices now. You don't have to stop and think about them, you just do them.

As we get started, let's make one thing clear. The goal of this book is not to fix something that is wrong with you. There is nothing wrong with you. In fact, your company, your family, your community, and the world need more of you.

THE NEW YOU

Do you feel confident that you know everything you need to know to be successful for the next 10 years? If you answered "yes" to this question, you are deluding yourself. The world is changing so fast that anyone who thinks he or she knows everything he or she needs to know to be successful for the next 5 years, let alone the next decade, is a fool. I know you're not a fool, so let's consider the next question: If you don't now know everything you need to know, then how are you going to learn? Are you going to go back to school? Probably not. School takes too long and costs too much, and the theories you learn there won't take you far in the real world we're living in. Are you going to read a book? Maybe, but what books do is give you ideas or understanding, and that isn't the same as the ability to take new action. Are you going to go to one of those one-day-wonder motivational seminars where you pay a bunch of money to see Tony Robbins, Zig Ziglar, or your favorite sports legend projected onto a mammoth video screen? That might make you feel good for a day or two, but then everything will go back to the way it was. Why? Because motivation is to the real development of potential as cotton candy is to nutrition. It's a nice treat, but no one ever got stronger by eating a diet of cotton candy.

The dilemma we are facing is that we have been sold a bill of goods about learning. In school, learning meant memorizing information, not putting it to use. As adults, we now think that learning can be reduced to acquiring new theories, models, tips, and techniques, simply by understanding them. It just doesn't work that way.

Your mind is not a computer full of circuit boards that can be rewired or software that can be upgraded. You might go to one of those motivational seminars, sit and listen and expect that you will be able to go back into life "reprogrammed," that at some moment the exact set of circumstances that were described in the seminar will occur, you will automatically know what to do, and you will spring into action. Even though of course it doesn't work this way, we keep doing it. We waste billions of dollars a year on programs, books, and CDs that not only don't work, but also *can't* work. Why not? Because that isn't how people learn!

The real tragedy in all of this is that it never occurs to us to question the entire structure of learning. Instead we start to question ourselves. We worry that we are dumb. *Maybe it's just me*, you think. It isn't just you! The entire structure is screwed up, and it is the source of most of the failings of our businesses today. We are going about the process of learning all wrong.

What if instead of dispensing theories, models, or techniques, we treated learning as the development of new competence? Our goal shouldn't simply be to understand; we want to put that understanding into action, to do better, feel better, be better. That means you need to develop new competence, whether as a manager, a parent, or a leader. You can only develop competence through practice, and practice takes time. While this may seem disappointing—who doesn't secretly wish for a quick fix?—you should be insulted by any suggestion that real learning can happen in an instant. After all, you've been developing your unique way of being human over the span of decades. You've invested a lifetime in becoming who you are. You can change, but not in an instant. The only way to authentically learn is through practice. Practice is critical to everything we are going to do. This is because the mind understands, but it's the body that learns. Understanding can occur in an instant, but authentic learning takes time. It is your body that lives and moves in the world, that takes action and has experiences, and the body can learn only through practice.

Consider, for instance, how you learned to drive. Did the state you learned to drive in permit you to just read the driver's manual and let you take the driving test? I don't think so. Did you watch a video of a NASCAR race, listen to an inspirational talk, then take the test? Not likely. Did you read inspiring little stories, sit in your room and recite affirmations, and perform visualizations of yourself at the wheel, then take the test? Of course not. You learned to drive by practicing under the watchful eye of a driving instructor—a coach—and by getting on the road and teaching your body how to do it. Initially it was awkward and scary, but your commitment to learning to drive was bigger than your commitment to being afraid. Let's say that last thing again, as it is critical. *When your commitment to learning trumps your commitment to being afraid, you will learn.*

The same is true for learning new practices of leadership, management, and life. Other books, tapes, and talks may point you in the direction of what you want to learn, but they can't teach you new competence. Only consistent, recurrent practice produces competence. If you adopt this approach to learning and commit to developing new competence and do the practices, then everything else will fall into place. Along the way, you will be inspired, excited, frustrated, and confused, and you may even want to quit. All of this is expected, but the new set of practices for learning that I am going to give you will enable you to move through all of this.

One of the critical new competences that you will learn is to mind your mind.

We all like to believe we are great thinkers, but what most of us call "thinking" largely consists of fantasizing, daydreaming, worrying, and scheming. We fantasize about romance, sex, sports, and celebrities; worry about health, money, and our waist size; daydream about winning the lottery; or scheme about how to exact revenge on the jerk who cut us off in traffic. Right now, for instance, even as you read this, your mind is probably wandering off, triggered to some random thought by one of the words above.

Your mind is like Grand Central Station. Thoughts roar through it like so many trains coming and going. If you aren't alert, you quickly become the directionless passenger helplessly hopping train after train. One minute you are in Grand Central, then the next thing you know you are off to Newark, then uptown, then downtown, then out to Queens, or some other unintended destination. Your thoughts ride you, taking you anywhere they want. The net effect is that you flit from thought to thought and have a limited capacity to stay focused on anything. Part of what we will do is show you how to focus your mind.

Another critical aspect of minding your mind is learning to manage the voices in your head. If you are sitting there saying to yourself, "What voices is he talking about?" that is exactly what I am referring to. Each of us has a chorus of little voices that are constantly chattering in our heads. It doesn't mean you are crazy; this is just part of being human. I liken it to a raucous congress that seems to be in constant debate about everything. While there can be a host of these characters, there is one, in particular, that I am concerned about. Most of us have a strong voice that tends to be very cynical. We will refer to it as your inner cynic or critic. This is the little voice in your head that is constantly telling you what is wrong with everything and everyone, especially you. He is the armchair quarterback who is quick to criticize every play you call, every move you make. He will tell you not to trust anything or anyone, to play it safe, keep your head down, not to take any risks. She is the judgmental parent, the one who will point out all of your faults, and when something goes wrong, she'll be right there with an, "I told you so—how could you be so dumb?" He's the boss always ready to tell you why your idea won't work, that the situation is helpless, and nothing you are going to do will make any difference.

Your inner critic does not want you to change.

We're going to do it anyway and one of the first steps in the process is that we are going to change the tone and texture of your inner critic. It isn't really possible to silence him or her but what we can do is make a big shift in how he sees the world and how you interact with him. Right now, you're thinking that that's impossible; actually, the little voice inside your head is jumping up and down and screaming that it isn't possible. (He has his own instinct for self-preservation!) You are going to stop living under his or her heel. But let's not be naïve; that voice has been with you for a very long time and isn't going to change without protest.

As I said in the beginning, this is a book for and about you. It will enable you to take advantage of the work that we have been doing for high performers in the athletic, military, and corporate worlds for the past 25 years. This is a book about how to conduct an internal transformation, one that actually produces an expanded version of you. It is about how you can authentically realize more of your innate potential as a human being.

The process we will use is simple. We are going to begin by learning about the nature and power of language, and about how we create our realities in and through language. With that foundation, we will then turn our attention to learning how to learn. No more settling for tips, techniques, and understanding;

you are going to learn the practices of authentic learning. Next we will build a basic centering practice that will serve you in whatever you do. After that, I am going to walk you through the Universal Performance Principles that we have found in high performers around the world. At the end of this process, you will have embodied a new set of practices, and in so doing discovered a different way of being human. You will move differently in the world and be the you that you always wanted to be.

To help you to get the maximum value from your investment of both time and money in this book, I have what I will call some strong suggestions. I can't require you to do any of this, but if you want to change, to truly transform, then I strongly suggest you do what I ask. The first is that you "do" the book. That means that you don't just read it, but also do all of the assignments that accompany each chapter. Reading it alone isn't going to produce the transformation you are seeking. It is a good first step, but not sufficient. That said, you do need to really read the book. While that may seem a bit obvious, I don't mean read it as you typically do, but read it with a new reading practice.

Most of what people call reading is merely passing their eyes over pages so they can say they have completed a book. They are then either disappointed because they didn't get any value from the experience or righteous as their inner cynic's point of view has been confirmed: "I told you this was a waste of time and money, but you wouldn't listen." If what you are up to is accessorizing your ego, then go through the book as fast as you can so you can be the first to brag to all your friends. If you are serious about your transformation, then a different approach is called for.

The first step is you need some skin in the game. Be clear about what it is you are looking for in your reading. Why exactly are you taking the time and expending the effort to read? What are you up to here? Curiosity is nice, but it won't raise you to your next level of development. You want to bring some ambition to your reading. You want to be looking for something, hungry for something, on the hunt for something as you read.

I want you to approach your reading as if you and I were having a conversation right there in your living room. Bring your concerns and ambitions clearly to the conversation. That way, when you read, you will insist that I provide you with the answers that you are seeking.

When you start a chapter, read it once very lightly. Skim it and see what jumps out at you. Then come back a bit later and read it again. This time, read it as if you were on the hunt for what you have your sights set on, being relentless in your quest. You will be surprised at how the chapter will show up differently for you on the second go-through. Don't just pass your eyes over the pages: Imagine that I am in the room with you and engage with me in the inquiry. We want to work together to produce this transformation and open a new future for you. Don't settle for being passive here. Take charge of your future and bring some power to your reading.

You may then put the book down for a day or two, do some of the practices that have been set out for you, then come back to it and read the chapter yet again. You will be surprised at how you notice things you didn't before, at how new meanings and possibilities show up. This is because you have shifted in the interim and are now a new and different observer of yourself, the book, and the world. That is exactly what we want. We begin to craft a new you by shifting the way that you see yourself and the world and by training you to observe things in a different manner.

The second thing I want to point you to is this: Rodale and HP2 are conducting an experiment. I have been building a unique body of work over the past 25 years, and Rodale has been building a highly effective way to reach and interact with its customers. In order for you to get the maximum value from my 25 years of work, we are going to enable you to get additional support via the Internet. We have set up a special Web site for readers of the book. If you go to www.thepowertotransform.net or the HP2 Web site, www.humanpotentialproject.com, and click on the link that is labeled The Power to Transform, you will find a window that asks for your name, e-mail address, and access code. Enter the code HP24U, and you will be granted access. Once inside, you will find all sorts of options for support. There are video clips, forums, and a place to subscribe to a newsletter. There are forms you can download to make your work easier and posts from people who are looking for partners to work with. You will also find that you are entitled to a discount on our live courses. All in all, it is a great way to get additional value from your investment.

Also, I suggest that you work in a team. All of our live work centers around the power of teams and communities. One of the big misconceptions about learning is that we can or ought to do it on our own. This is a big mistake, as it is way too easy to either delude ourselves into thinking we are doing great or to dupe ourselves into making an overly negative assessment of our progress and giving up—probably something you have done before. Human beings learn best when they are part of a small team or community of committed learners. In this way, there is always someone outside of you who can see you more clearly than you can, someone to inspire you when you feel resigned, and someone who can see the way forward when you are stuck.

Instead of taking the book and reading it alone in your room at night, you will get the most value from the ideas and process if you have other people to go through it with you. We have set the Web site up to facilitate your working together, including a forum for people who are looking for partners. Don't be bashful—be bold! Your new future is at stake.

Finally, a word about the assignments. As I said earlier, you aren't going to learn anything just by reading the book. The key to your transformation is to do the assignments at the end of each chapter. Remember, authentic learning is the development of new competence, and the only way to develop competence is through practice. At the end of each chapter you will find an assignment designed to build your competence in the material presented in the chapter.

This is as direct as I can be: If you don't do the assignments, then you're not going to change and there will be no transformation. In fact, if you don't do the assignments, then you run the risk of having things worsen (or feel worse), as you will become more cynical and resigned. I trust that is clear.

As noted above, you will make the most progress if you do the work with a partner or team. However, the assignments are designed for you to work with someone or on your own. Either way, it is critical that you do them! Do them like they matter, because they do. Don't do them with the dutiful and grim approach you probably took toward your least favorite school assignments. We aren't in school, and procrastination, cramming, and trying to "get by" with the minimal possible effort won't work here. Your future is at stake.

Along the way, there are going to be times when you will get bored and frustrated, and you will want to quit. These are normal reactions to the prospect of authentic change. Don't let them deter you. Be committed to your goal of shaping a new you. Do the work and be sure you pace yourself so that you can make steady progress without overwhelming yourself. Depending on your level of ambition, you can move through the entire process in roughly 90 days. That means that you can do parts of the assignments for multiple chapters at the same time, as they all call on you to do some reflection and that takes time.

Be careful though as it will be a mistake if you set out to do them all at once. You run the risk of feeling overwhelmed, and the point of the process is to generate a transformation that produces permanent change, not to get through it as fast as you can. If you do the assignments in fits and starts, that is okay, as long as you do them.

This is my prelude. If you have read this far, you have seen the possibility, you have the appetite, and I have the means and the methods to satisfy it.

THREE

LANGUAGE SHAPES REALITY

> WORDS DO NOT LABEL THINGS ALREADY THERE.
> WORDS ARE LIKE THE KNIFE OF THE CARVER.
> THEY FREE THE IDEA, THE THING, FROM THE
> GENERAL FORMLESSNESS OF THE OUTSIDE.
> AS A MAN SPEAKS, NOT ONLY IS HIS LANGUAGE
> IN A STATE OF BIRTH, SO IS THE VERY THING HE IS
> TALKING ABOUT.
> —ESKIMO QUOTE

In the first section of this book, we are going to build a foundational set of new practices for you. The next three chapters are devoted to practices that will form the foundation for everything else we are going to do. It is imperative that you not only understand them, but also work to bring them to life. Your intention to change your life has brought you this far. You bought the book, you read my introduction, and if you didn't read the last chapter on how to get the most out of the book, then go back and do that now, before you proceed. This is the point where the work of creating a transformation begins.

As I said earlier, the process of shaping the new you is simple—

not complex. That doesn't mean it will be easy. While the process isn't complex, it will require considerable effort on your part, and this is the point at which you need to step up. So when you are ready, let's go!

I am going to start with something that may at first seem a bit daunting or irrelevant. I ask that you be patient for just a bit, as I am confident you will see why we need to start here. Philosophers call what we are going to talk about *ontology*. Ontology is the examination of the basic nature of being and existence, how we as human beings experience ourselves and our world. I know, a certain cynical little character in your head is probably saying that you are no philosopher and asking what this has to do with your transformation, with the practical work of building the new you. The answer is absolutely everything. After you grasp a few basic principles of the ontology of language, we will be able to move with purpose and focus toward the goal of building your new future. Let's go ahead and get philosophical for a minute.

Over the last several millennia, those of us in the Western world have been conditioned to believe that reality exists independently, outside of us. Reality, in this traditional view, is something "cold" and "hard" that happens to and around us. According to this school of thought, we "accept," "face," or "confront" a reality that we had no hand in creating, and over which we have minimal control. This is a belief system that has been developing for hundreds of years and which we now tend to simply accept without question.

However, a new view of reality supported by research in the fields of linguistics, physics, neuroscience, systems analysis, and computer science makes a different claim: Human beings actually shape their own reality, and language is the tool that we use to do it.

The old view held that people use language merely to describe reality. But humans are creatures that swim in a sea of language. It is as essential to who we are and what we do as the air that we breathe is to our physical existence. In this book, one of our foundational building blocks is the claim that language not only describes reality, but it also literally **creates** reality as well. In other words, we shape our experience of the world by the stories and narratives that we tell ourselves.

The Human Potential Project also holds that language is not merely a function of the mind, but also of the unified mind and body. It is a *somatic* phenomenon. Our bodies shape and are shaped by the stories that, over time, form what we know as our realities. To be sure, language does indeed serve to describe the world. There is a world of objects out there. More importantly, though, it also has a more fundamental, powerful, and generative capacity; this generative capacity will form the foundation for a new, expanded version of you, your world, and your future.

Let's take a brief look at how this all came about and where we think it might be taking us.

In prehistoric times, humans' capacity for language evolved as a competitive advantage in a world in which we lacked the size and strength of many of the competing predators. With language we could coordinate with our fellow humans in a way that wolves, lions, and other creatures couldn't.

Over millennia we developed the means to communicate in writing as well, allowing our words to span time and distance. With writing came the development of logic, as people could now see and share ideas and distinguish myth from reality. The 17th-century French thinker Rene Descartes represented the epitome of the rational philosophical system, in which being human—being alive—is inseparable from thinking. *Cogito, ergo sum.* I think, therefore I am. In this view, reason is what makes us human. The Cartesian model has formed the cornerstone of Western culture for the last 400 years, and although this system still holds sway, its hegemony has been challenged in recent decades.

Incubated at major universities such as Harvard, Stanford, MIT, and the University of California, and encompassing the fields of philosophy, psychology, biology, and systems analysis, a new wave of thinking is slowly bringing the Cartesian epoch to a close and producing a radical new understanding of human beings and our behavior. The Cartesian system was based on the study of rationality, the stripping away of the irrational to reveal the immutable truth.

But more recently a new view, based on the ontology of language—the idea that language creates reality instead of merely describing it—is emerging to take its place.

Why does any of this matter? Because we are alive at a critical juncture in history. We have entered a period of major transformation in human communication: the advent of electronic technologies that have created the mediums of global communication and community. This new age was presaged by technologies such as the telephone, radio, television, film, and the photocopier, and is now blossoming with the exploding use of computers and cell phones, as well as the global rise and reach of the Internet. Within the span of two generations, our vast world of different nations, languages, and cultures has evolved into the global village that was envisioned in the 1970s.

It is easy for those of us living today to lose sight of the fact that, for most of our history, physical distance was a seemingly impenetrable barrier to human interaction. In the last century, it has been reduced almost to the point of irrelevancy. Something similar has occurred with the concept of time. Even in the recent past, for example, it took 20 hours to travel from New York City to Beijing. Doing business with someone in China was, therefore, complicated by time and distance. Now, with e-mail, text messaging, and other communication technologies, the residents of both cities are neighbors living in real time in the same virtual metropolis.

This global shrinkage has produced a dramatic acceleration in the pace of change. In the last few decades we have witnessed a revolution of products, ideas, economies, styles, and political movements, once tethered by distance and time. To use the now-common phrase, our world has become flat, and it moves at net-speed.

For millennia the status quo ruled, and change was a rarely tasted spice of life; now change forms our daily staple. When I was a boy in Spokane in the 1960s, I remember how the pace of change dizzied my parents: color TV, a man on the moon, rock and roll, touch-tone phones, riots in the cities. While all of this seemed normal to me, because I had never known life without these things, it seemed as if they couldn't imagine the world spinning any faster. From the perspective of today, of course, the pace of life in the '60s seems a bit pedestrian. Fifty years from now, perhaps, the pace of today's contemporary life will seem equally quaint.

The point of all of this is that we have created a world that moves at a pace our bodies were not designed to contend with. Our biology has not developed anywhere near as fast as our technology. In a week we can now have more input and stimulation to our nervous systems than people experienced in a year just 2 centuries ago. We have created our world with language, and if we are going to successfully adapt to the revolution in communications, the flattening of the world, and the epidemic of change, we must grasp the generative nature of language. It is the key to our collective future and the key to your transformation.

Because this idea is so important to the work we're going to be doing together, let's be clear about how humans use language to generate their realities. I don't mean that you can simply announce, "I won the lottery!" and make it true. That would be magic, and we're talking about how language shapes *reality*, not fantasy. And yet a new world opens up when we see the possibilities we hold when we truly comprehend the generative power of language.

Let's turn to shaping a deeper understanding of what I mean when I talk about language and to building some basic practices in this new realm. I will begin by teaching you what we call the basic linguistic moves, then show you how we use these moves to construct and make operational the principles that will enable you to take your place in this new world.

When I talk about language, I am not talking about a specific language such as English, French, Chinese, Spanish, or Hindi. I am talking about the phenomenon of language. All languages contain the same linguistic building blocks, and I refer to these as the *basic linguistic moves*. What this means is that whenever a human being opens his or her mouth to speak, he or she is making one of these moves, regardless of what language is spoken.

The basic linguistic moves are:

- Declarations

- Assertions

- Assessments

- Requests

- Promises

- Offers

That's it. That's all there is. There may be a million words in the English language, but no matter how you mix, match, or configure them, you will be making one of these moves.

Once you begin to see that these basic moves construct your world, entirely new realms of possibility will open up, and actions that you would have thought impossible will become commonplace. Read any magazine, newspaper, or book, and all you have are various combinations of these moves. Once you come to see them clearly, you will be able to perceive things that others don't, laugh at some of the pretentiousness around you, and be very clear about what is unfolding—how language is in that very moment shaping reality. Stay with me and watch what happens. Here is how these basic linguistic moves work.

DECLARATIONS

Declarations are statements that generate action, set new directions, and name things. In the absence of a declaration, nothing ever happens. They can have a huge impact, "We are going to invade Iraq!" or little consequence, "I am going to Starbucks." What matters here is the authority of the person making the declaration. If President Obama declares that we are going to invade Iran (at this moment he hasn't done that), then troops and materiels will start moving. If former President Clinton declares that we are going to invade Iran, people will just look at him strangely and wonder if he has lost it. He no longer has the authority to make that declaration.

You have the name that you have because your parents had the authority to declare your name. Judges declare that you are guilty or innocent; priests and justices of the peace can declare that you are married because they each have the authority to make those declarations. A central point here is that as human beings, we always have declarative authority over ourselves. You ultimately declare all of the choices that shape your life. While you may opt to give it up, and governments are constantly trying to usurp it, one of your birthrights as a free being is your declarative authority over yourself.

ASSERTIONS

Assertions are statements that we usually refer to as facts. They can be true or false, and are always oriented to the past or present, never to the future. To be a "true" assertion, it must pass what we call the universal observer test. This means that anyone on the planet, no matter what country he or she is from, would agree with your assertion. Grass is green, water is wet, the sky is blue, and 2 + 2 = 4 are all things that a universal observer would attest to. After that, the list starts to dwindle. When you apply the universal observer rule, you will find that there are very few things that you can assert. There just isn't that much *truth* out there.

We can assert things only about the past or present because these are the increments of time that we can observe: They have occurred or are unfolding in the moment. The future hasn't happened yet, and thus we can't assert anything about it as fact. There is strong evidence to suggest that the sun is going to rise tomorrow, but we can't state that as an assertion because much as we might all want it to, there is no certainty until it actually happens.

ASSESSMENTS

Assessments constitute the bulk of human speech and communication. These are our opinions, feelings, thoughts, sensations, and personal points of view, and are the building blocks for our interpretations of the world and characterizations of each other. While we spend a lot of time dishing them up, assessments are useful only for designing action, and it is their relationship to action that gives them power. Assessments open and close possibilities for action, and people act out of their assessments, not their assertions.

"Sales are down from this period last year" is an assertion. For now let's assume that we can pull out the comparative sales charts and prove that it is true. So what? The answer to that question depends on your assessment. In and of itself, the statement doesn't drive any particular action. The chief financial officer may assess that this means we need to cut spending and thus he would predictably propose a cost-cutting plan. The head of sales may assess that it means we aren't doing enough to generate business, so we need to spend more on sales initiatives. Which one is right or true? Neither, as *assessments are never true or false*. They are what we call grounded or ungrounded. Grounded means that you can provide assertion-based evidence to support your assessment, and ungrounded means that you cannot. The CFO may base his assessment on his years of experience and the claim that he has been through this before. The head of sales may base her assessment on a comparative analysis of financial performance as driven by research on proportionate investment in sales initiatives over time. Does that make her assessment true? No, it means that it is grounded, but no matter how much grounding you have for an assessment, no matter how much you may like it, or how many people agree with it, it is never true. This is critical, as you will soon find that most of who you think you are is a construct of ungrounded assessments. Moreover, you will discover that much of what you have always assumed to be the truth or facts about life and our world are merely assessments that have been masquerading or sold to you as assertions.

Unlike assertions, assessments can be oriented toward the future. "I think it is going to rain tomorrow," "I think the market is going to tank," and "I am sure the sun will be up in the morning" are all assessments. They may be grounded, but they can never be true.

Here is why this matters as we work to build the new you. Outside of your physicality—your height, weight, gender, eye color, hair color, and age—there is nothing that we can assert about you that is true. Everything that you think of as your immutable character or nature is all a collection of assessments. You may think, or others may tell you, that you are kind, gracious, attractive, sexy, smart, generous, lazy, or self-centered. None of it is true, not the parts you like or agree with, not the parts you don't like or deny. None of it is true, as they are all assessments. They may be grounded or ungrounded, but they are all *always just assessments*. Again, the reason we need to wake up to this is because assessments open and close possibilities, and *human beings act on our assessments, not our assertions*.

We shape the way we act and treat one another based on our assessments. Let's say you are at a party, and a friend of yours introduces you to someone named Jim. You look Jim up and down, and what I am going to call your assess-o-matic starts up. This is something that human beings do. We are constantly assessing everything and everyone. It is a survival mechanism that was very useful when we were hunting on the savannahs and needed to assess whether someone or something new was a potential threat or not, but now that we have evolved beyond that, it isn't necessary in many modern situations. At the party, it kicks in and the little voice in your head begins reeling off a series of assessments. "Hmm, tall, not too heavy, doesn't look very threatening, has a funny mustache, I am sure that I am smarter than him, etc. . . . " Your friend goes on to say, "Jim is a great guy, and I think you will have a lot in common as you both like to ski." *You both like to ski* sounds harmless enough, but even this assessment will open certain possibilities and close others. It opens the possibility of an interesting conversation about skiing, a potential new ski buddy, and the opportunity to share insights on the best resorts. At the same time, it may close the possibility of a conversation about snowboarding, surfing, or bowling. They may not be permanently closed, but they fade into the background in the presence of the assessment about skiing.

It is important to note that assessments are not innocent. When you gossip about what a jerk your co-worker is, those around you are shaping an assessment, not just of him, but of you too. They will act on their assessment that you are a gossip and not to be confided in, despite the fact that they come to you for the latest dish. Moreover, your casual, "innocent" assessment of your co-worker can have unintended consequences. People aren't used to grounding assessments. They often just accept them at face value and move with them. When a new project comes up, one that your co-worker would be well suited to, he might never get a call, as someone took your assessment at face value and didn't even offer him a shot at it. Your assessments are not innocent. Each and every one opens and closes possibilities, even when they are about you.

REQUESTS, PROMISES, AND OFFERS

Requests, Promises, and Offers are all elements of what we call action cycles. These are the moves that people make when coordinating action together. A promise exists when someone that we call a customer makes a *request* of someone else, that we will call a holder, to take some specific action or produce some specific result by a specific moment in time and the holder *promises* to do so. An *offer* is simply a cycle in which the roles are reversed and the holder initiates the conversation. There is an entire body of work that we call **Commitment-Based Management** that is built with these basic moves. This is a fundamental part of the work that we do with corporations. An entirely new world opens for those leaders and managers who grasp the power of managing commitments as opposed to the standard practice of managing activities and see that what we call an organization is in reality a complex set of nested action cycles. These are deep and rich waters for those who want to embrace their careers and ensure the viability of their organizations.

There you have the basic linguistic moves. That's it, that's all there are! Again, my claim is that whenever a human being opens his or her mouth, he or she is making one of these moves. With these basic moves in hand, we can turn our attention to some of the key principles that enable us to see how we use language to create our realities.

1. HUMAN BEINGS LIVE IN A WORLD OF INTERPRETATION

By virtue of the way that our brains, nervous systems, and bodies work, it is impossible for any single human being to know "the truth" or reality in any absolute way. We can know only how we observe a given incident or situation. What we are most often blind to is that what we think of as an observation—an unbiased record-ing or memory—is actually an interpretation. As you just saw, an interpretation is merely a set of assessments, and as such, cannot be true or real in any absolute sense.

Consider the example of a minor automobile accident, a classic fender bender. Two cars approach an intersection controlled by four stop signs. The cars appear to arrive and stop simultaneously. Instead of one car yielding, both proceed into the intersection, where the vehicles collide at a low speed. Neither driver is injured; both jump out of their cars and confront the other driver with their version of the incident.

"I got to the intersection first. I had the right-of-way."

"That's not true. I got here first. I had the right-of-way."

"Nonsense!" the first driver says (he may likely use a stronger word). "We even made eye contact. You gestured for me to go ahead."

"I did no such thing. I was adjusting my rearview mirror. And besides, you were talking on your cell phone."

As the two motorists continue their futile argument, a pedes-trian who witnessed the accident is solidifying his own view of the incident: Neither car came to a full stop, both proceeded into the intersection at the same time, and both drivers are equally at fault.

Which version of the accident is true or real? The two drivers look at the incident from radically different perspectives, as does the witness. All three parties are certain that they know what really happened. What they have, instead, are three different interpreta-tions of what happened, of what reality is.

Now consider the example of a televised debate between two presidential candidates. During the writing of this book, we were in the final stages of the Barack Obama/Hillary Clinton race. I have two friends who are passionate, lifelong Democrats. Janet had been thrilled by Senator Clinton's performance during the matchups. In her view, Clinton was better prepared, more articulate, had better defined policies, was quicker to respond, clearly more experienced, and, in sum, obviously superior. This was Janet's reality. She was therefore shocked to find that Jack had an entirely different version of the same debates. He was impressed by Senator Obama's passionate articulation of a new vision for the country, his commitment to staying on the high road in terms of campaign style, and, as he wasn't part of any old guard, his promise to clean house in Washington. According to Jack, Obama not only won the debates, but he was also clearly the superior candidate. According to Janet and what she insists are completely objective standards, Clinton was the unequivocal victor. To her, Obama supporters have been blinded by charm and charisma and have lost touch with reality. Where is the true, objective reality here? Clearly there isn't one.

There is a tree in your yard. About that there is no dispute; the tree is real. But what is real about the tree? Is it tall or short, broad or thin, bushy or scrawny? Are the branches beautiful or ungainly? Are the leaves brilliant with color or mundane in their ordinariness? It all depends on your point of view, your interpretation. A lifetime of input and experience molds our interpretations and shapes our standards, and the only thing we can say about them with certainty is that they are all different. As human beings, we each craft our own reality.

This is why we must let go of the notion that any one of us possesses the "truth" about anything. An interpretation does not contain or reveal the truth. What it does contain is power, the capacity to open and close possibilities for action. The pedestrian witness's interpretation concerning the fender bender, for instance, determined the ruling of the insurance adjusters working the case. Janet's interpretation of the presidential debate determined how forcefully she supported her candidate and opposed the other.

The notion that supposedly concrete and irrefutable truths and facts (including some of the ones we hold most dear) are only *interpretations* may at first seem threatening, but rather than limiting our options or undermining our confidence, this realization can have the opposite effect. It puts our view of reality on a sturdier foundation. It opens the possibility for consistent, coherent, designed action, and that is exactly how we are going to construct the new you.

Instead of a fixed reality, what we have are interpretations, and these interpretations are constructed from language.

2. LANGUAGE IS GENERATIVE

Language brings forth reality, in that what we say or don't say shapes who we are and the events around us. How often have you observed, either with rue or relief, that events might have turned out differently had you only spoken up, or had you simply shut up? A simple declaration or assessment can shift events dramatically. The absence of that same statement leaves things to continue on their existing path. Let's look at some simple examples.

"I am going to the store." A simple declaration, but in the absence of that declaration, even if you make it only to yourself, no trip is going to happen. You may have a conversation with yourself in which you debate the necessity of going to the store, the timing, the purpose of this trip, but until you make the declaration that you are going, nothing will happen. Your declaration generates the new reality of a trip to the store.

Now let's look at a more complex example, one that is near and dear to us all: romantic love. When we say, "I love you," what are we doing? We are making a declaration. Once we make that declaration, all sorts of possibilities open and new actions flow. But let's take a different look at love, which may seem to you to be "true." When people ask you why it is that you love your sweetheart, you will reply that he or she is beautiful, intelligent, funny, charming, sexy, and, I hope, the list goes on. If we use the basic linguistic moves, we find that what we have is a set of assessments.

To you they may feel like the truth or assertions, but they are just assessments. If you were to describe your beloved to someone who didn't know her, or who knew her in some other context, that person might be baffled by your description. Why? Not because they "don't really know her," but because they have a different experience of her, and their different experience has generated different assessments. In addition, they most likely have a different set of standards by which they make their assessments. We all know that beauty is in the eye of the beholder. It is in this way too that language generates our reality.

Let's go one step further and look at a bigger example. Some years ago I was living and working in Seattle when a few independent coffee shops started opening up. These were little boutiques that offered a "European" experience of drinking coffee. Most of us weren't too clear as to why we needed a new coffee-drinking experience. Back then, coffee was something that you bought in a big can from the grocery store or purchased for pocket change with a meal. It was a bit bitter and typically needed cream and sugar to make it palatable.

Starbucks was one of the boutiques, and we were all quite amazed to learn that its management intended to expand around the city, and then take the company public and expand it nationally. "Coffee shops? You have to be kidding—who needs one of those on every other corner?" The answer is no one. No one *needs* one. So what did Starbucks do to create a demand, a sense of need? It began advertising. What does advertising do? It creates a new story; it opens new possibilities. What was the possibility here? You could have a new experience of drinking coffee, a more European experience. They created the sense that without this you were missing out on something that not only tasted better, but is also much more sophisticated and cool. As Americans, we are deeply interested in keeping up with current trends, being sophisticated, and above all else, being cool.

In brief, Starbucks shaped a story in which one could step into a new world. The price of entry? Just a few bucks. The story the company told is built of nothing but assessments. But remember, people act out of their assessments. Watch how this unfolded. Our assessment was that going to Starbucks offered a new possibility; our assessment was that the price for stepping into this new world was minimal; our assessment was that the risk of being either disappointed or embarrassed was minimal. Our declaration was that we would go and check it out. As we now know, millions of people shared these assessments and made the same declaration. Whether you like Starbucks or not, what is important to understand is that what the consumer bought first, what caught our attention and moved us to act was *the story*, not the coffee. We bought the story, and the story is a linguistic construct. It lives in language, not the world of things. This is how language shapes our futures.

In each of these examples, you can see how language generates reality. To be clear, I am not saying that everything that exists does so only in language. There is indeed an external reality independent of language. In the sphere of human enterprise and interaction, however, we have a unique, language-based capacity to invent ourselves and our futures.

When we speak, we shape our identity and the events that surround us, and this is exactly how we are going to shape the new you.

3. ACTION GENERATES BEING; YOU BECOME WHAT YOU DO

This might sound like an obtuse bit of Zen Buddhist philosophy, but I assure you it is much more than a word game or a riddle. In fact, the final principle is perhaps the most important, as it has a direct bearing on how we can change who we are. Understanding the implications of this statement will shift the way you see the world and move in it.

One of the most limiting relics of the historical, rationality-based perspective of life is the idea that what we call "the self" is permanent and immutable: "I am the way that I am, and there is nothing that can be done about it." In this view, a person demonstrates who they are through his or her actions, and once established, that identity will never significantly change: "He behaves that way because that is just the way he is."

Let me give you an example. Let's say that my friend Fred happens to act in a way that those of us who spend time with him assess to be mean and selfish. We would therefore naturally say that Fred is a mean and selfish person. It naturally follows that he acts mean and selfish because he is mean and selfish.

This traditional method is a rational and even reasonable means of understanding people: By observing a person's actions, we draw conclusions about how they act and who they are. At the same time, it is also limited and one-dimensional. The new view of people and language holds that our actions, in addition to shaping our identities (who we are), also allow us to transform ourselves. By repeatedly acting in new ways, individuals can move in a new direction and release old ways of being. In this way, we can invent who we are in the world by taking new action. This is the key to creating the new you.

This next piece of insight I'm going to offer may throw you a little, but stay with me. One of the other relics of the old Western tradition is the notion of the "true self." How often have you heard or said something to the effect of, "If they only knew the real me, how I really am, they wouldn't think or say that." We tend to believe that there is some inner true "me" that only I really know, that I have some true identity that I reveal only to those who are closest to me or in some cases to no one at all. This is a notion that we are deeply attached to, and thus there are hundreds of books that will help you to find, love, dialogue with, heal, express, nurture, and ignite your true self. Here is the part that will rock you a bit: There is no such thing.

Think about it. In this story of the true self, there is apparently some little, tiny mini-me that lives in my heart or in my head and is the genuine, authentic me. We all know that if we were to open your head or heart, we'd find there is no little character in there pushing buttons and pulling levers. The you that you think you are doesn't exist. Let me say that differently. Who you *say* you are doesn't really matter. Your identity isn't who you say you are; it is who others say you are that matters. I know, that's rough—let's go again. Our identities are not composed of the distorted or fantasy-blurred interpretations that we cobble together about ourselves. Instead, *our identity consists of the series of assessments that others make about us, and these assessments are based on our actions.* The truth of it is that you are the last person that we ought to listen to when it comes to assessing you. Your personal assessments are hopelessly biased either strongly for or strongly against yourself. Despite what you may want to believe, your assessment of you ought to be near the end of the list of those you listen to.

Sit with that for a minute, and let's go back to my friend Fred. He decided he didn't like being known as mean and selfish, so he read a dozen books on becoming a more compassionate person. He then attended a seminar that got him in touch with his deep inner capacity for caring and generosity. For days after the seminar he spent time each day visualizing himself as a caring and generous guy. The problem was that he continued to act in a manner that was interpreted as mean and selfish. Because his behavior didn't change, despite all the reading, seminar sitting, and visualizing, he will continue to maintain the identity of a mean and selfish guy. Fred continues to be baffled and chagrined by this assessment. When we speak to him, he certainly doesn't see himself that way. In fact, he regards himself as reserved and prudent. Fred's identity in the community, however, is not driven by his self-assessment. His identity is the collective assessment of his community. And assessments live in language.

This may be a bit disorienting, and that is in part intentional. I intend to shake up your understanding of reality, especially your notions of who you really are. At a deeper level, though, I hope it proves to be liberating, because this is where the power to change yourself and your life lies.

Contrary to our traditional belief, Fred is not doomed to living out his days known as a mean and selfish guy. If he can accept that others don't see him as he sees himself—reserved and prudent—that they instead assess him as mean and selfish, and if he can change the behaviors that shape those assessments, then he can begin to do something to shift his identity. If Fred repeatedly acts in a kind and generous manner, then, over time, his community will observe these actions and change its assessment. This is how Fred can transform into a kind and generous guy. No amount of reading, meditating, visualization, or anything else is going to make a difference.

We are what we do, not what we think. We are the product of the stories—told in language—that others form about us, and they form these stories based on what we do—not what we think!

By working over time to take new actions, any and all of us can form a new identity. Sally, a manager who is consistently late for her sales-department meetings, has built an identity as being unreliable and flaky. This is typically not a career enhancer. However, if Sally commits to taking new actions and consistently shows up early or on time for all her meetings and appointments, she will eventually build a new identity for herself as being reliable.

This is how one becomes what one does. You can't consistently show up on time for meetings without being reliable. It isn't possible. Your new actions generate a new identity and a new way of being. It doesn't matter what you are saying or thinking to yourself. That inner voice isn't the one to listen to or be guided by. By acting in a way that is consistently reliable, punctual, and responsible, you become those things. There is no way around it. This concept may sound simple, but its implications are profound.

Indeed, it forms the cornerstone of our work: In order to change ourselves, we must change our *actions*, not our minds. By changing our actions, we change ourselves.

Your capacity to change is directly tied to your willingness to learn the basic linguistic moves. Everything that we do will come down to various combinations of these moves. With a new declaration, a new future opens up. Without one, all we are left with is a continuation of the status quo. You are here now because you have declared the status quo to be unacceptable. That means it is time to get to work on your transformation, so here is your first assignment.

Our goal is to begin to build your competence in recognizing and using the basic linguistic moves. The first step is to develop your capacity to see them in action.

ASSIGNMENT #1

FOUR SECTIONS
TOTAL TIME TO COMPLETE: 3.5 WEEKS

You are now at a critical stage in the process. You have done some reading, which is a great start, although as I have stressed from the beginning, reading alone isn't enough to generate your transformation. You have to do the work, and this first assignment is where the work begins. Now you get to decide. Are you serious about having a different future or just looking to accessorize your ego with another merit badge? Building a new you is going to take time and perseverance. Don't treat this like a buffet table and just do the pieces that you like, or that seem easy or entertaining. Do it all and you will see the real change happen.

Here is how we begin to build. If you are working with a partner or a small team, you will want to coordinate a series of meetings so that you have a structure for your learning community. To get the most out of the process, I suggest that you plan to check in with your learning team once a week for the first month. After you have some experience in supporting each other, you can decide if you want to maintain that schedule or check in more often. To get some help with this, go to our Web site, www.thepowertotrans form.net, and you will find some guidelines for setting up a learning team.

Whether you are working on your own or with a partner or team, the assignment is the same and has four sections.

SECTION #1

For the next 10 days I want you to buy a daily paper. I would prefer that you not purchase the same one each day, but if different papers are all you can get your hands on, so be it. If you have access to your local paper and the *Wall Street Journal*, the *New*

York Times, or *USA Today*, that would be great. What you are going to do is pick one or two front-page stories each day and read them. Keep a highlighter handy and hunt for the basic linguistic moves. In particular I want you to find *complete sentences* that are assertions—not a few words or phrases, but complete sentences. We have been told that what the papers contain is the news, the facts about what is going on in the world. We have been conditioned to believe this, but as you will find, there really aren't many assertions in the news at all. Instead, there are assessments masquerading as assertions or, said another way, opinion pretending to be fact. I am not just talking about the editorial pages; they are clearly dedicated to assessments. You are reading the "news" sections.

Experience tells me that you will be fortunate to find more than a few assertions in any news story. Remember, what we are training you to do is to become a much more keen observer of your world and the way language shapes it. That means you want to be alert, and avoid being lulled into settling for partial sentences. Again, if you want to see some examples of what I am pointing to, check the Web site as there are some highlighted stories you can look at.

So that we are clear, I am not saying that the news ought to report only the facts. First of all, there aren't that many, and we would have a lot of dead air time and blank pages. Nor am I suggesting that there is some grand conspiracy to distort the truth. Instead I am enabling you to see the basic linguistic moves in action and to see how they shape our world.

Take, for example, a hypothetical story about some natural disaster. The facts might be limited to the following three assertions: The wind blew down 10 houses; five people were killed; 50 people are now homeless. But no news story, not even on the Weather Channel, is going to settle for that. Humans love drama, we crave engagement, and we want to feel things. So instead of a factual report, you will get pages of human interest—assessments made to look like assertions.

So read a news article, note the absence of assertions, then start marking up the assessments and make some written notes on what sort of emotions they evoke in you. Do you feel sympathetic toward people, angry at government bumbling, annoyed that they were so foolish? Exactly what emotions do these assessments evoke?

For 10 days I want you to do this practice. Make *written* notes about what you are observing, what emotions you notice as you read, and which of the linguistic moves you can see. A quick side-bar on notes: When I ask you to make some written notes, what I am up to is getting you to crystallize your thinking. Having notions running around in your head doesn't mean you are thinking. By driving you to write, I am pushing you to slow down, make some connections, and formulate them into a coherent narrative. This is how you actually make sense of things, and I want you to be able to see how you make your particular brand of sense out of things. With that in mind, let's turn our attention back to the news. In general you will find the news to be rich with assessments, scattered with a few assertions, and occasionally you will find a request. Make notes on what actions you feel compelled to take when you read. This is important, as I want you to clearly see the connections between language, emotion, and action.

After 10 days, when you have developed a basic capacity to see the linguistic moves, I want you to go back and read your notes and see how what you notice has shifted and then write about what you see and how it moves you. Write some comments on what you make of all of this. If you are working with a partner or a team, set up some time to share your notes with each other and see how your perspectives as a group have shifted.

From this point forward, you will be a very different reader of the news, of magazine articles, government reports, corporate reports, and the world.

SECTION #2

Now we are going to go a bit deeper with the practice. You can do the rest of the assignment while you are doing the first piece, but don't be in a big hurry to get it all done. We aren't in school here—you're not rushing toward a degree—so give yourself some time to really work the assignments, as we are now in the actual process of creating a new you, and you don't want to shortchange yourself by hurrying through it.

The next thing we are going to work on is grounding your assessments about yourself. Over the course of the next few days, I want you to pick five assessments that you have of yourself and want to work on changing. These should be critical or negative assessments you have been carrying deep inside yourself for a long time. Our goal is to shed some light on them and free you of them.

Examples would be statements that start with: "I'm not good at," "I'll never," "I'm too . . . " or any other self-defeating pronouncements. For many of us, these are private and deeply held, so much so that they may even be unarticulated. A helpful step can be to recall some moment in your childhood in which you remember someone saying something to you that you can still feel, still remember, or may otherwise have taken on. For each of these assessments, I want you to ask the following questions and *write down the answers:*

1. What is the assessment?

2. What domain of action does it exist in? "I am a terrible dancer" is domain specific and could be grounded. "I am a klutz" is what we call a *universal assessment* and as such is always ungrounded. Go for something specific.

3. How long has it been with you? Can you remember when it first showed up?

4. When you think about or feel this assessment, what mood or emotion does it evoke?

5.   What purpose does this assessment serve? We hang on to them for a reason. It might be to be right about something or to play it safe by not risking something. If I hold that I am a klutz, then I don't need to bother risking the embarrassment of being a beginner at snowboarding, as I believe I know how it will turn out.

6.   Who first delivered this assessment to you? You may think that you did, but very often we hear it first from someone else.

7.   What standards are you using to make this assessment? Would the rest of the world or the community that knows something about the domain of action agree, or are you making up your own standards? One of the ways that we set ourselves up for failure is by using what we call fantasy standards, perhaps the most dangerous of which is perfection. Perfection is a loser's game—all you can do at it is lose, as nothing and no one is ever perfect, and you aren't going to be the first. Often we suffer as a result of inflicting fantasy standards on ourselves. We are particularly adept at this when it comes to assessing our looks and bodies. Brad and Angelina are fantasy standards.

8.   What possibilities does your assessment open and close? All assessments always open and close possibilities. If my assessment is that I am a lousy dancer, it may open the possibility of learning (learning is always open, regardless of what you may think) by taking lessons, and it may close the possibility of entering the tango contest this weekend.

9.   Where does it live in your body? This may sound a little peculiar, but if you pay attention and develop awareness, you will discover that assessments do indeed live in the body. As you write about each of your assessments, you will notice that somewhere in your body you can feel that it has a location.

10. Finally, you have to determine if your assessment is grounded. Remember, grounding means you have some assertions that you can provide as evidence. Most of the time you will find that these assessments, these deeply held stories about yourself, are completely ungrounded.

Take some time between the assessments that you choose to work with. Don't rush through all of them just so you can say you did your assignment. That isn't the point. The goal is to begin to feel something shift inside you as you let go of the ungrounded, negative assessments that you have been hanging on to. In some cases, families have handed these assessments down—often unconsciously—from generation to generation. These are not the kind of heirlooms you want to keep!

Once you have worked your way through five assessments, make written notes on what you observed about how you responded to the process. If you have partners, share your notes and experience with them. If not, keep moving.

SECTION #3

The next phase is a continuation of the last one, only this time you are going to work on five positive assessments that you have of yourself. Remember, whether negative or positive, assessments do not tell the truth about you. As human beings, we work very hard to avoid negative assessments and equally hard to receive positive ones. Our goal is to free you from the grip of assessments, positive or negative.

Do the same practice that you just completed on at least five positive assessments you have of yourself. Work through the same 10 questions, and in addition to writing down the answers to the questions, take notes on what you observed about your relationship to positive assessments. How does your body respond to them? Was it easier or harder to work on them? What do you see about the possibilities that your positive assessments open or close? Keep your notes to share with your partner or hang on to them, as we will come back to them later.

SECTION #4

The final piece of the assignment may be a bit simpler. After you have completed your newspaper reading, I want you to spend the next 2 weeks engaged in a new practice of observing. As you go about your daily life, I want you to pay attention to the conversations around you. I want you to see how readily you can identify the basic linguistic moves in action. For a few days, see if you can listen for declarations. They may be simple, such as "I am going to the store," or more complex. The key is to begin to hone your skill at distinguishing them. For the next few days, listen for assertions. There won't be many, but try to spot them. After that, notice the sea of assessments that surrounds you on a daily basis. In each case, pay attention to your body. What does it want to do when you hear each of these moves?

From there, pay attention to the requests people are making all the time. Do you notice this? Can you hear the offers around you? Make some written notes on all that you observe and what you are beginning to see about the generative capacity of language. Keep them in your archives, or share them with your partners.

One last thing—have some fun with this! You have completed your first assignment: The transformation has begun, and you are on the way to real change.

FOUR

LEARNING
IN A NEW WORLD

> IN A TIME OF CHANGE, LEARNERS INHERIT THE
> EARTH, WHILE THE LEARNED FIND THEMSELVES
> BEAUTIFULLY EQUIPPED TO DEAL WITH A WORLD
> THAT NO LONGER EXISTS.
> —ERIC HOFFER

You are reading this book because you have the desire to become more of who you know you can be, to realize more of your human potential, to design and deliver your own transformation. The only way to do that is to change, and that means you have to learn new ways of being and moving in the world, new ways to carry yourself, and new practices to achieve your ambitions. This may seem both obvious and simplistic; of course learning is the only way forward. Sounds great, but when you get down to the nitty-gritty of how to learn, you hit a wall. It's not as if you haven't attempted to learn in the past. However, learning something new never seems to be as easy—or as easy to put into practice—as you were led to believe. Let's see if I can show you why that is and what to do about it.

Learning is one of the fundamental, defining activities of human beings. We live in language, and we have a vast capacity for learning. This is part of what makes us human. Given the universally acknowledged importance of learning, you would think that we would spend considerable time and resources understanding how it actually works. Unfortunately that isn't the case. While we have any number of academicians spouting theories, our educational system (with its traditional scholastic model for learning) continues to be highly ineffective. Learning, according to this tradition, is an intellectual process that consists of the passive acquisition of theories, facts, models, ideas, and information. In this tradition, you memorize all of the above to accomplish the goal of understanding, as we are deeply attached to the belief that to understand is to know. It's time that we stop blindly following the tired, largely dysfunctional models that we endured, with varying degrees of misery, during our school days, and that we now pass on to younger generations. It's time for a new model of learning.

I propose a radically new interpretation and a revolutionary set of practices. Our view turns the old system on its head, as we hold that learning is a function of the whole body, not just the mind. Rather than launching yet another futile attempt to memorize facts or information to facilitate intellectual understanding, we claim that learning is the active process of developing a new competence, a new capacity for action. In this chapter, we'll discuss the fundamentals of what we call *authentic learning* and identify the enemies of learning: the self-imposed limitations that undermine your capacity to learn—and your future.

Let's begin by defining our terms.

Authentic learning is the process of developing what we call *embodied competence. Embodied* means you can take the new action without having to stop, think about it, or look it up in some book. The new action is ready at hand when needed. *Competence* is simply the capacity to consistently produce the desired result.

The true test of learning is not whether you can parrot back some fancy new lingo that you picked up in a book or in a course; it is whether you can consistently perform a new action, both now while you are working with me or another teacher, and in the future, when you are out of the classroom and in the world. Understanding might come in a flash, but learning occurs through consistent practice over time.

Authentic learning is the process of developing embodied competence, and practice is the only way to develop competence. This is the part that nobody wants to hear, so I will say it again. The only way to develop embodied competence is via practice. Everyone wants to play in the championship game, but no one wants to go to practice. Let me be as clear as I can about this. It is not possible to learn without recurrent practice. You can understand, but you won't learn.

Before explaining all of this in detail and warning you about the enemies of learning, take a trip with me back 20 years to my first encounter with Dr. Fernando Flores. The episode will clearly illuminate the difference between authentic and traditional learning, and between embodied competence and intellectual understanding.

By 1988, my company had achieved striking results with AT&T; I was busily building our roster of clients and solidifying the practical and philosophical groundings of our work. As I made my professional rounds, I kept hearing about Dr. Fernando Flores, a man who seemed legendary and larger than life. He'd been born and raised in Chile, where he'd shown early genius in the fields of engineering and economics. A protégé of Salvador Allende, he was heavily involved in the profound social and political changes taking place in Chile in the early 1970s. When Flores was only 29,

Allende appointed him the nation's minister of finance, and he eventually became secretary of state. He went to work one day in September 1973, and didn't come home for 5 years. Imprisoned by the dictator Augusto Pinochet, he suffered years of deprivation and hunger, finally gaining release through the efforts of Amnesty International, then American secretary of state George Shultz, and Stanford University. With their help he landed in San Francisco at the age of 40, broke, with no job, and with a wife and five children to support.

With the assistance of the above-noted granting agencies, Flores went back to school and earned a multidisciplinary PhD. His doctoral committee consisted of professors of management, philosophy, and linguistics from Stanford and UC Berkeley. Flores's dissertation, *Management and Communication in the Office of the Future,* and a book that he wrote with Dr. Terry Winograd, *Understanding Computers and Cognition,* have become classics in the information technology and management theory worlds. In the early '80s, Flores predicted the rise of the World Wide Web and the shifting nature of the way we interact with computers. Most importantly, he clearly articulated the notion that language shapes our reality. He developed software designed to improve workplace effectiveness by managing the linguistic moves I showed you in the last chapter, and he set about building a software company. However, he quickly found that in training people to use the software, he was actually training them to reconsider their lives. This prompted him to create a new business in which he offered a series of courses that began with showing people how to design their lives. This evolved into courses on leadership, management, business, and even love. After much procrastination, I finally carved some time out of my schedule and went to see what he was all about at a business seminar he was leading in Berkeley, California.

The seminar took place at a hotel in the Berkeley marina;

seagulls flew over the pier, and the skyline of San Francisco jutted out of the fog rising across the bay. In front of 200 people who'd traveled here from all around the country, Flores took the stage. He is a powerfully built man: thickset with a droopy mustache; dark, piercing eyes; a heavy Spanish accent; and a fiery temper. It soon became clear that he had no interest in feeding our self-esteem or indulging the comforting stories that we'd constructed about ourselves and the American way of doing business. He wanted to wake us up by shaking us up. His style was anything but gentle.

At the time, I was in my mid-thirties and full of self-confidence. I'd been successfully working with AT&T, Microsoft, Intel, EDS, and other corporations, making a name for myself and the company by bringing about transformational change in the business world. Lately I'd been studying the subject of inspiration and thought I'd reached some fresh insights on how it functioned in the process of motivating people and generating productivity. So when Flores started talking about his ideas for mobilizing groups and individuals for action, I decided to question him.

"What do you mean by 'inspiration'?" Flores shot back, his dark eyes boring into me. "How does it work? Where does it come from? Can you show me some? Would you like to demonstrate it for us? Go ahead and inspire the room."

As I sat there with all eyes riveted on me, I felt confident, as I had been reading a lot about inspiration of late. I stood up with only a bit of trepidation. After all, I'd been doing great with my own audiences and assumed that for a few minutes I could hold my own on Flores's stage. I was seriously wrong. Under his withering cross-examination, I proved hapless and helpless. Within a few moments, I was completely lost. I thought I knew something about inspiration and teams, but in that moment none of it made any sense, none of it was available to me, and I was reeling in a sea of embarrassment, so far off center that I couldn't even see it from where I was. The net effect of this was that I found myself having a curious out-of-body experience as I watched myself artfully being taken apart.

What Flores showed me was that while I might have "known" what I was talking about when I used the word *inspiration,* there is a big difference between knowing or understanding something and being able to do it. (*This would have been all the more fascinating if I hadn't had to learn this embarrassing lesson in front of 200 people!*) In that moment I came to clearly see the difference between embodied competence and understanding. I may have understood the idea of inspiration from an intellectual standpoint, but I had very little competence in demonstrating it. My purpose now is to provide you with a similar insight while sparing you the experience of having to learn your lesson in front of 200 people. Trust me, you will like this much better.

There are two fundamental points to make about competence. Confusion on these points often produces big messes, bringing you, perhaps, to your equivalent of my Fernando Flores moment, but distinguishing them clearly can help open the path toward authentic learning.

1. COMPETENCE IS DOMAIN SPECIFIC

When we say that someone is competent, we are saying that he or she has the capacity to consistently perform to some accepted standard in a specific domain of action. We get ourselves into trouble when we assume competence to be universal as opposed to domain specific. That someone is competent in one domain says nothing about his or her competence in another.

LeBron James, for example, is a virtuoso basketball player. This doesn't mean he's good at baseball, golf, or tennis. Nor does it mean that he's a good basketball coach, or that he's good at driving a car, managing a business, or being a father. Likewise, that someone is a good surgeon doesn't mean he knows how to run a hospital; that someone is a good engineer doesn't mean she's a good project manager, and that someone's a good salesman doesn't mean he's a good sales manager. An excellent rock-and-roll drummer might have no idea how to play jazz. As a society, we tend to fall into the trap of assuming universal competence. That he was a great coach doesn't mean we should elect him to congress. That he was a brilliant scientist or software engineer doesn't mean he can run a company. That he cashed out with millions because he was part of a start-up that took off doesn't mean he is a brilliant investor. Competence is domain specific.

2. COMPETENCE AND CHARACTER ARE NOT THE SAME THING

When we say a person is competent, we are assessing her capacity to act in a specific arena. This does not mean she is a "good person," as we are not assessing her morals or character. By the same token, when we say a person is incompetent, we assess his incapacity to act in a specific area. We're not saying he's a "bad person." By judging competence we do not judge character, personality, or the person's inherent worth as a human being. Most of you are currently incompetent in the new practices that I am introducing you to. Does that mean that you are lazy, dumb, or stupid? No. It simply means you have not yet devoted the time it takes to embody the new practices, to become competent. Think for a moment about the people in your life whom you have labeled with those terms, and you may suddenly see something new about them or even yourself.

Let's turn our attention to the process of authentic learning. Life constantly dishes up opportunities for you to learn. The dilemma is that we don't always see them when they are in front of us. Thus while we clearly choose to learn some things, often we find that the desire to learn arises only out of a breakdown. This happens because as human beings we are resistant to change and don't know what we don't know. Authentic learning therefore often begins when we find ourselves being a *bull in a china shop,* a person who is blind to the realm he is moving in and makes big messes without even realizing it. The proverbial bull doesn't recognize that he is in a china shop, knows nothing about china and crystal, and has no concept that he is in a place where he needs to be extra careful not to break anything. Instead he hears the crunching and shattering, and he panics. At some point in your life, you have been the bull in the china shop, as have all of us. In this situation, awareness arises in one of two ways. Either someone who cares enough about you—or the china shop—takes you aside and points out the nature of china and china shops to stop you from continuing to make such a mess, or else the mess you make is so big that you finally "fall face down" into awareness. Whether someone else alerts you to the mess you're making or you come to this awareness yourself, this dawning of awareness is universally accompanied by a two-word declaration: "Oh shit!"

We all have these moments. It's part of being human. What matters is what you do with them. Every one of these moments provides what I call a choice-point: a point at which three choices become available to you. Two of them are powerful and one of them is popular.

The first powerful choice is to be what we term *self-declared ignorant.* I know this may not sound too powerful, but here is why I say that it is. Humans have been developing for hundreds of thousands of years, and for most of that time we lived in nomadic clans and tribes. Thus for most of human history it was possible for someone to know all there was to know. In prehistoric days, you could learn all that you needed to get you through your entire life by the time you were 10 years old. This was easy to accomplish because there wasn't all that much to know. You learned to hunt, track, skin, cook, use plants, make tools and weapons, and track the passing of the seasons, and that was about all you needed to know to thrive as a member of a nomadic tribe.

Over the last few hundred years, our world has developed considerably, and in our stupendously complex modern world it is, of course, preposterous to hold the same ambition. No one can be universally competent. Instead, we choose a few domains in which to invest the bulk of our time, talent, and energy. Other aspects of life, however, while outside our competence, still require our attention.

For example, I know that there is a vast body of knowledge, regulation, and law known as the Internal Revenue Service Code. I have no commitment to learn in this arena, but nonetheless I have to be responsible for my taxes. Thus I declare myself ignorant and delegate my tax preparation to someone who is competent. I hire a tax accountant, who has declared himself a learner in this domain, to act on my behalf. If you look at modern life, you can see countless examples of this phenomenon. Not so long ago, lots of people worked on their cars. These days, you need to be a computer scientist, electrical engineer, and mechanic to do work on a car, so we delegate. We do the same with doctors, lawyers, and all of the other service providers in our lives. Declaring oneself ignorant in a specific domain can be a powerful and dignified move.

We get ourselves into trouble when we refuse to make this move. This brings us to the second of the three choices. This is the popular as opposed to the powerful one, and that is to be what we call being a *pretender*.

The pretender is the person who, instead of acknowledging his lack of competence, tries to conceal both his incompetence and his lack of commitment to learn. He is the guy who reads all the self-help books or goes to all the courses and picks up and uses the new jargon, but develops no new practices. In sports, the pretenders buy the latest gear and trendy fashion items, but never take lessons to improve their game. Instead of seeing them working to improve on the courts, greens, or slopes, you find them in the bar wearing their new gear and talking a great game. In business, pretenders read all the popular books, attend all the motivational seminars, and listen to all the tapes, but never seem to change their behavior. They look and sound terrific at cocktail parties as they spout the lingo, but inevitably fail where it matters, on the job.

Despite negative consequences to relationships, finances, and physical well-being, the pretender makes no commitment to learn. He goes to the gym and lifts a few weights so he can brag to people that he works out, but he never engages in a serious fitness program. We have all seen these characters in our lives, and, truth be told, we have all likely been this character at some point. Despite the obvious downsides to this, why is it so popular? In part because we are lazy, in part because we are afraid, and in part because we are deeply invested in being cool.

When you come to your choice-point and are serious about learning, start the process of authentic learning by becoming a *beginner*. This is the most powerful move you can make as a learner. To be a real beginner is to make all three of these clear declarations.

1. *I see there is a realm in which I am not competent, and I commit to learn.* In other words, I am not going to pretend that I know something I don't, put up a false front, or act like I don't care. Instead, I am going to be committed to the process of authentic learning.

2. *I am going to authorize someone to coach me.* This is very important, as it moves you away from the dysfunctional tradition of thinking you are going to learn on your own from tapes, or via the Internet. You can get awareness of what you want to learn from these mediums, but authentic learning occurs

only inside of a structured developmental process (like this one) and preferably under the watchful eye of a competent coach.

3.   *I will be at peace with being a beginner.* This is perhaps the most difficult thing for adults to do. Why? Because as a beginner you are new to the activity, and as such you will be making all of the beginner's mistakes, and that isn't cool! This is where you repeatedly cross your ski tips and fall on your face, your tennis serve looks more like a home run, and your first attempt at a soufflé looks more like a tortilla. As most adults are much more committed to looking cool than to learning, we typically don't learn much in our adult lives. Then we are shocked or indignant when the world passes us by.

I know this sounds simple, and that's because it is: simple as in not complex. But it isn't easy. It takes effort. Being an authentic beginner proves very difficult for most adults, and I am no exception.

As part of my own practice for honing my edge, I make a point of learning something new every few years. This is important for a host of reasons, not the least of which is that it prevents what I call psychosclerosis. You know about arteriosclerosis, the hardening of the arteries. Psychosclerosis is the hardening of the attitudes that tends to overtake adullts (yes, the *dull* is intentional—this is what happens when psychosclerosis takes hold) who stay stuck in a limited set of life experiences and skills.

With that in mind, I make a practice of learning something new every few years. A few years ago I decided that I would learn to snowboard. I was already a fairly accomplished downhill skier, but I'd decided to break out of my winter-sports comfort zone and, in my late forties, learn something new. Knowing my own aversion to being a beginner, I committed to learning in this new domain by renting a condo for a long weekend at Schweitzer Mountain Resort, in northern Idaho, and not bringing along my skis. I paid for 4 days of private lessons in advance, as I knew what was likely to happen. Sure enough, I spent the first few days either on my face or on my butt. My harsh inner cynic was going full blast: "What are you doing, what are you trying to prove, you can't do this, you are going to kill yourself, what if someone sees you, why, at your age, are you paying all this money to endure torture and embarrassment?" Like I said, I am no different from you in that regard. But my commitment to learning was bigger than my commitment to being cool, so I hung in there, choosing and constantly re-choosing to be at peace with being a beginner. For the first few days I would curse the little kids whizzing by me on the bunny hill. "Ah ya little punks, you should see me ski!" I thought. By the end of the weekend, to my great satisfaction, I was making my way down all but the roughest runs on the mountain.

Once you take the most difficult step and declare yourself a beginner, you can then move with peace into the world of authentic learning, the process unfolds, and you move up through the levels of competence. It is important that you understand how authentic learning really works. You start as a beginner and spend a lot of time with a coach. With continuous practice and skillful coaching, you move out of being a beginner and become a novice, competent, proficient, virtuoso, and, with a lifetime of work, eventually a master. It is important to understand that most people will never get past proficient at anything during their lifetimes. That doesn't mean they are poor students: It is merely a commentary on how much effort it takes to build virtuosity, let alone mastery. These are rare states of achievement, and most people simply aren't willing to put in the time to get there—and, to be clear, I am not advocating that you should.

As a last note on the process, it is also important to understand that authentic learning doesn't occur on a curve, as we have been led to believe. Instead it is more like a set of very steep stairs. You work and practice, and just when you are convinced you aren't getting any better, you make the leap to the next level, and the process starts all over. A simple way to understand this can be seen in the graphic that follows.

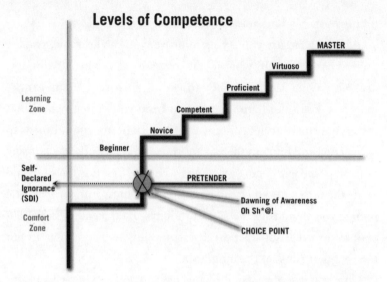

The key to all of this is your constant willingness to be a beginner. Every time the game changes, your most powerful move is to start with what we call a beginner's mind, to look at the new possibilities and learn your way into a new future.

THE ENEMIES OF LEARNING

Much as I wish it were not so, the truth is that there are forces at work that are committed to making sure that you never learn. I call these the enemies of learning, and they are the most dangerous kind of enemy. You can't see them and you can't touch them, but they are deadly, as they live in your mind. They are the stories that you tell yourself about yourself. They claw at your commitment and undermine your ambition. The only way to fight them is to recognize them for what they are: fear-based blather that your inner cynic dishes up to keep you stuck right where you are. Once we shine the spotlight of awareness on them, they will scurry away, but you have to stay vigilant, as they will be back. Let's start with identifying them and then talk about what to do about them.

1. *Knowing.* The number one enemy of learning is knowing, or more precisely, the assumption of knowing. This is the

automatic response of, "I already know this," that arises whenever you are exposed to something new. The mind quickly goes to, "This is just like X, and I already know that." This is a great way to close off possibilities, as once you know something you tend to quit paying attention.

2. *The unwillingness to be a beginner.* As we just noted, the most critical first step in the process of authentic learning is the willingness to be a beginner and to make all three of these critical declarations:

- I commit to learn.
- I authorize a coach to instruct me.
- I am at peace with being a beginner.

3. *Being blind to our blindness.* All of us have blind spots in the ways in which we view and meet the world. We can't understand, comprehend, or visualize that which we are blind to. We need someone to help us. Several years ago, for example, an episode of *The Sopranos* dealt with the vicissitudes of Artie Bucco, the owner and chef of Vesuvio, the Italian restaurant frequented by Tony Soprano and his friends. In the show, we see Artie taking great pleasure and pride in schmoozing the guests at Vesuvio; he mistakenly thinks the customers love his cornball jokes and discomforting personal attention. When his business nose-dives, Artie examines every aspect of the restaurant except his own behavior. Finally, in a difficult but necessary act of friendship, Tony tells Artie the truth. The scales fall from Artie's eyes, and he is no longer blind. When he goes back into Vesuvio's kitchen, the customers return to the restaurant.

At times we all require an outside observer to shed light on our blind spots. These blind spots are normal, natural, and common, but they limit us. Books, lectures, and recordings can help us see new possibilities for learning, and so can asking a friend or co-worker for an honest assessment of our actions.

4. *The desire to be comfortable.* In an authentic learning process, comfort is the enemy. Human beings demonstrate a powerful, deep-seated craving for comfort in all its forms:

physical, intellectual, and emotional. When confronted with new ideas, most people react strongly. When our familiar patterns, associations, and responses are challenged, often we respond with fear and anger. Our minds cling to stability and predictability, and we tend to judge something new as dangerous.

The notion of learning and changing, moreover, always looks good from a distance. In fact everyone is in favor of learning, as long as it doesn't mean me and it doesn't mean now. When presented with our own opportunities for change and growth, however, discomfort arises. The array of excuses, dodges, and delays we toss out can be astonishing.

In short, beware of the perfectly natural desire for comfort. Unfortunately, comfort and authentic learning are mutually exclusive.

5. *The insistence on understanding everything all the time.* Any new idea or practice seems difficult, complicated, and unclear, simply by virtue of being new. And yet, along with our desire for comfort and safety, we also crave understanding, falling prey to the notion that clarity yields safety and certainty. When an unfamiliar situation lacks clarity, we tend to label the agents of change as "wrong."

"If the coach really knew what he was talking about," the quarterback grumbles after practice, "then this new offense wouldn't be so confusing."

"If this is so great, then it should be easy to understand."

In both instances, a person grants himself permission to dismiss the new practice and retreat into the comfort of the familiar. That retreat closes the possibility for learning.

6. *Confusing opinions with learning and confusing awareness with competence.* An opinion is not the same as a thought. Human beings endlessly churn out opinions about every aspect of their lives. This is natural and normal, but it's not the same thing as thinking. Thinking is the process of generating an original idea or distinction. Thinking requires energy and attention; having an opinion requires neither. Under the sway of our opinions, moreover, we wall ourselves off from learning as

we think that because we have an opinion about something, we must "know" it.

A related enemy appears when we confuse awareness with learning; we mistakenly assume that a new awareness automatically equates to a new competence.

For example, hoping to ease tension in her marriage, Jane attends a class on building communication skills. During the first session, it dawns on her that her husband resents the manner in which she speaks to him. Shocked to discover her error, Jane decides to change; she'll never talk to her husband like that again. Despite the valuable insight, however, Jane has not yet learned the skills for more effective conversation. She goes home after that first class full of resolve, but her awkward attempts to engage her husband fail miserably; he seems only to resent her more. Jane has confused awareness with learning. The attainment of awareness and the development of competence are two entirely different processes. The main failing of most personal or professional development work is that it settles for providing you with awareness as opposed to building new competence.

7. *Addiction to fast food or the magic pill.* This is the characteristic disease of our times. We want it all, and we want it now. The disorder is especially prevalent in the business world. The necessary competencies for today's managers and executives have grown increasingly subtle, sophisticated, and complex. The process of developing genuinely new management practices requires months and often years of work. The more senior the executive, the more deeply embedded her style, and the longer it takes to learn and change. It's foolish to assume, for instance, that any 2-day corporate retreat can prove sufficient for reshaping practices that have taken decades to establish. Indeed, presuming such instant change to be possible can cause lasting harm to individuals and organizations.

Deluded by the zeitgeist of instant gratification and the failure of our society's established learning practices, we have fashioned our own traps. In the business world, executives doubt the usefulness of training and education; they engage in programs more out of political correctness than a belief in their utility. Given this attitude, it's little wonder that companies typically limit such efforts to the 2-day retreat. "It's not going to produce any concrete results, so why devote more time to it?" the executives reason, thus enacting a self-fulfilling prophecy.

At best, these 2-day intensives raise awareness. They might even impart a few tips and techniques. Achieving competence, however, requires authentic learning, and that takes time. However well intentioned, the habit of falling for the latest short-term, magic-pill program will result only in long-term failure.

As individuals, we see little evidence of improvement or real change as we constantly move from book to book, teacher to teacher, and course to course. Most of these don't have much more than a few anecdotes or tips and techniques to offer, so there isn't much more to be had. However, if you want to really learn, then you need to get past the quest for the magic pill, the latest and the greatest, and work to build new practices.

8. *Forgetting the essential role of the body.* In confronting this major enemy of learning, we make a radical departure from the conventional wisdom. We claim that while the mind understands, it is the body that actually learns. Let's illustrate this key point with an example from sports.

Tom, an avid golfer, constantly seeks to improve his game. While watching the Golf Channel one night, he happens across a show featuring Tiger Woods demonstrating his chip-shot technique. Tom, of course, would love to chip like Tiger Woods, so he turns up the volume and sits forward on the couch. He listens carefully, jots a few notes, and even takes a few phantom practice swings right there in the living room. The next day he goes out to the course and eagerly pulls out his pitching wedge. Tom tries mightily to apply Tiger's precepts, but, to his disappointment, his chip shots still slice into the bunkers rather than feather onto the green.

What happened? Tom intellectually understood Woods's suggestions; he knew he had to adjust his stance, change his grip, and shorten his swing. Tom's mind grasped these concepts; but it is his body that must make the adjustments, and the body learns in a different manner than the mind. The mind accumulates information, generates understanding, and experiences insights, but the body learns only by recurrent practice. Through consistent practice embodiment occurs, and only when we have achieved embodiment can we claim to have learned. In order to chip like Tiger Woods, Tom first needs to make peace with being a beginner. Instead of merely watching the Golf Channel, he must take lessons from the pro at his local course. In order to embody a Tiger Woods–like swing, Tom will have to hit thousands and thousands of practice shots, just like Tiger did. This is a level of commitment that most citizen-golfers simply can't make.

Or consider an example from the realm of business. Committed to developing better leadership skills, Alice, a midlevel manager, studies books and attends lectures on the subject. Alice mentally grasps the concept that a good leader must be willing to take risks, and resolves to practice risk-taking by having a long-overdue conversation with one of her employees, a loud, physically imposing man who is habitually late for work. But the next morning, when the man again arrives late at the office, Alice looks the other way.

Why? Not because she doesn't understand the concept, but because risk-taking entails dealing with fear, and fear lives in the body. Alice has not yet built practices for coping with fear. Thus, she doesn't have any new behavior available when fear arises.

The mind understands, but the body learns.

9. *The drive for novelty.* Similar to the quest for the magic pill, the drive for novelty can be debilitating and, ironically, undermine your future. If you're constantly on the hunt for something new, after all, you'll never focus your time, attention, and energy on the long process of developing the competence that will deliver authentic change. Under a media bombardment touting the latest fads, theories, and systems, the lure of the next big thing at times proves overwhelming.

In the business world, this enemy shows up as the "buffet table" approach to training. We take a bit of Tom Peters, a dash of W. Edwards Deming, a habit or two of Stephen

Covey's, a notion from Warren Bennis, a theory from Peter Drucker, lash it together with some Six Sigma, spicy quotes, and colorful PowerPoint slides, and voilá! The result is a "greatest hits" training program. Lacking coherence, however, the patchwork program fails to deliver. It's like trying to build your dream car by cobbling together the front end of a Ferrari, a BMW's drivetrain, a Jaguar's suspension, and the body and interior of a Mercedes. With no unifying design or structure, the result is a very expensive piece of junk instead of a dream car.

Yet we continue to cling to a blind, unreasoning faith in novelty. The pressure to appear up-to-date is especially intense in the corporate world. When one of these hybrid learning systems flops, as it inevitably must, a company's human resources department scrambles after the next fad, and the cycle repeats.

If I want to learn karate, I find a good teacher and work with her consistently, usually over a period of years, to develop my technique. I don't study karate for 6 weeks, aikido for a few months, and kung fu for a year and expect to develop competence in karate. Nor can you learn to be an effective leader by chasing after every new interpretation that comes along or trying to cherry-pick tips and techniques from a host of teachers. The same is true in the transformation you are undertaking. If you genuinely want to develop a new you, then stay with me while we go through the process. You won't get anywhere trying to pick a few pieces from me, something else from another book, and yet something more from a tape series.

10. *Living in constant assessment.* This enemy is very crafty, as it works in two ways to close off the possibilities of learning. Here is how it works. You are exposed to something new. Your mind's first response is to assess or judge it. The most common and basic assessments are:

I like/don't like this.
I agree/disagree with this.

These simple, automatic assessments close down the possibilities for authentic learning. If I like something, then I tend to quit listening as my mind moves quickly from liking to knowing: "I like this because it is like X, and I know X is true." Similarly, if I don't like something, then the mind tunes it out: "I don't like this, therefore it must be wrong; if it is wrong, then there is no reason to pay attention."

The same thing takes place with agreeing and disagreeing. Either assessment tranquilizes us into closing down the possibility that there is anything new to learn. If I agree, then there is no reason to keep paying attention, because I know what she is saying to be true. If I disagree, then there is no reason to stay engaged, as this guy is obviously an idiot, and who needs to listen to an idiot?

11. *Characterization.* In the presence of this enemy, we make up stories about ourselves and the world, and confuse these stories with reality. We seize upon our incompetence in a single domain, for instance, and cement that into the foundation of who we are. But as we explained earlier, lack of competence does not equate to a lack of character. The fact that I can't seem to hammer a nail straight doesn't mean that I'm dumb, lazy, uncoordinated, or incapable of learning.

Far too often, we use a simple beginner's mistake to start a story that begins with the line, "I can't do this. I'm too old, too young, too busy, too fat, too uncoordinated. . . ." The ways to fill in the blank are endless. This self-sabotaging statement is often followed by another: "I'm not smart enough, I'm not fast enough, I'm not good enough; it's too late for me."

Another variation on this narrative goes: "I can't learn that; it's too sophisticated, too complicated, too technical." Common to all these statements is one underlying, unspoken theme: There's something wrong with me. This unfounded interpretation, which chokes off learning and stunts our growth as human beings, is no less tragic for being so common. That it happens is a part of life. That we let it stop us from living the lives we want is no longer acceptable.

All of these enemies of learning have likely attacked you at one time or another. Like the rest of us, you are probably more vulnerable to some than to others. While fierce and relentless, these enemies are at the same time as insubstantial as shadows. Rather than manifestations of reality, they are elements in a story of our own creation, and as we now know, we can change our stories and our actions, and in so doing, we can change ourselves.

Here is a final note on learning. One of the mistakes we make is to believe that we can or should learn on our own. This is dangerous for a number of reasons. First, it is too easy to fall prey to ungrounded assessments about how we are doing and delude ourselves into thinking that we are making great progress or that we really suck when neither is the case. In addition, the reason that we typically attempt to learn on our own is that we are embarrassed to be a beginner in public. This too is a big mistake. Authentic, sustained learning is an inherently social process. We learn best and most easily in a community of committed learners. These are people who will support you when you want to quit, provide useful assessments of your progress, and share insights and lessons with you. This is why I advised you to find some friends or partners to go through this process with. I want you to have your own learning community, as with that support you are likely to have the most success.

As you also know by now, learning is inherently challenging and takes place only through practice, patience, and perseverance. Indeed, these three qualities are the hallmarks of a committed learner. The only way to embody a new competence is through recurrent practice. Practice takes time and requires patience. The committed learner must continue to practice, persevering through doubt, weariness, negative assessment, and the occasional rotten mood. All of these are much easier in the presence of a committed team, a community of learners who share the same ambition and commitment. Let's turn to your second assignment.

ASSIGNMENT #2

THREE SECTIONS
TIME TO COMPLETE: 2 TO 3 DAYS

SECTION #1

The first thing we are going to do is inoculate you against the enemies of learning. They are always working against you to sabotage your future, so we need to attend to them. The best way to do that is to simply put your attention on them. Sit down and write some notes about which of the enemies of learning is most likely to get you as you begin to move forward. "None of them" is not an acceptable answer. No human being escapes all of the enemies of learning, so get to work and focus your attention. This process should take you at least 15 to 30 minutes, as I want you to focus attention on the subtleties of the enemies. In what sort of situations do different ones grab you? What can you do when they show up? What new declarations can you make in the face of these enemies?

Once you have made your notes, have a conversation with your partner or team about them. If you are working on your own, save them, as we will come back to them later.

Much as I would like to tell you that doing this exercise will keep you safe from the enemies of learning, that just isn't the case. As you go through this process, they will continue to grab you, and in many cases with increased intensity, the further you get. They don't want you to change; they don't want you to grow; and they aren't going to go away quietly. You are going to have to be vigilant as we move through our work together. They will be back, I promise.

SECTION #2

The next piece of work has to do with making some assessments of yourself. As we noted above, competence is domain specific, and what we are going to do is train you to make some grounded assessments. Pick five activities that you say you have some skill at. It doesn't matter what they are. Examples would be cooking, driving, any sport, card games, sales conversations, whatever you choose. For each of the activities, assess your level of competence and ground your assessments. As you should by now expect, you are to do this in writing.

Let's assume that you pick cooking. That is too broad of a domain. There is a very wide range of types of cooking. Are you good at Italian, French, Mexican, Japanese, Greek, or Indian? Each of these is very different, so hint number one is to be sure you have a specific domain. Next, let's see your standards. If you say you are proficient at cooking Mexican food, then you ought to be able to prepare a wide variety of Mexican dishes without much assistance from either a coach or a cookbook. You can do beans from scratch, make your own tortillas, move easily from meats, to fish, to sauces. You know your spice rack, and you are assessed by other cooks who are proficient or better to be proficient. Make some notes that detail your standards and the grounding for your assessment in each of the five domains you choose.

When you have completed this work, again share your notes with your partners or team. If you are working solo, save them, as we will come back to them.

SECTION #3

The final step is to make some declarations about something you want to learn. I am content to have you commit to learning the practices that are contained in this book, as that is why you bought it in the first place. If you want to take on something in addition, then go for it. Making the commitment to learn in this case means writing down what it is, in detail, that you want to learn. Being a better person is not specific enough. I want you to think about standards again. From your perspective, what does your transformation look like? How will you know when you are complete? What are you willing to do to accomplish your learning goals? What are you going to do when the enemies of learning assault you, as they most certainly will? Who are you going to grant permission to assess your progress? How much time are you going to devote to your learning? What might you have to give up to make it all happen? When you have your notes complete, have a conversation with someone about what you have written. Don't be afraid to get some comments that you may not like or agree with. Many of us still fall into the trap of thinking that we can do it by magic, that it will all happen in an instant. If that is what you are expecting, then you bought the wrong book. I am going to produce real results for you, because you are going to do some real learning. Get your outcome clear, your standards set, and your commitment firm, and let's keep moving!

FIVE

IT ALL MOVES FROM CENTER

EXPECT NOTHING—
BE READY FOR ANYTHING.
—SAMURAI ADAGE

In 1989 I traveled to Africa, making a pilgrimage of sorts with 10 other human potential practitioners from the United States. For more than a decade, my colleagues and I had been nudging, prodding, and occasionally dragging individuals and organizations out of their comfort zones, encouraging them to take risks and adopt new practices. The members of our group weren't burned out; on the contrary, we were invigorated by our work, but we knew that to remain fresh and authentic, we had to recharge our batteries by probing our own limits and living by our own standards of learning.

We wanted to put ourselves on the line, journey to a place that was both unfamiliar and extreme, that would awaken all of our senses. We wanted to find a place on the planet that was still wild, while there was still some wildness to be found. Our organizer, Dick Leider, knew of three brothers, sons of missionaries, who ran a guide service called Dorobo Safaris in the East African nation of Tanzania. It was sort of an African version of *Bonanza*— the three Peterson brothers living in their compound in the heart of the wild.

One of the brothers is named David, but he quickly became Tarzan to us. He was lean and fit like the fictional character and insisted on heading into the bush wearing a Masai tunic and sandals, toting a World War II–surplus backpack, and carrying an old Enfield rifle. Despite his unorthodox appearance and flamboyant style, David was an excellent guide who knew the country intimately. His missionary parents had brought him and his brothers there when they were kids, and he grew up with the peoples, languages, and animals of Tanzania. Our charge to him was to find us a place where no foreigners had been before— someplace so remote, we would be the first non-Africans to set foot on it. After scouting out the region by airplane, he suggested a trek up the Great Ruaha River in southern Tanzania. He warned us that the journey would be physically challenging and potentially dangerous. We replied that challenge and danger were just what we were after.

We arrived in Arusha, which is in the north of Tanzania, and found ourselves in a different world. The sights, the sounds, the smells, the air, the light, the rhythm and energy of the land were all completely new to us. We spent the first few days getting used to being in Africa. We went to the markets; we toured game parks; we ate the food and drank in the experience. We got ready.

The second portion of the trip was a 10-day trek through the remote parts of the Masai Land. Our guide here was a Masai chief that David had known since they were boys together. At 39, the chief was younger than many of our party and could speak English, Masai, and Swahili, which was two more languages than any of us could claim. For 10 days we trekked up and down the hills of the Masai country, where the temperature soared every day. I barely noticed the discomforts, however, because I was having a terrific time, although not in the manner that I had expected. Instead of being pulled out to the edge of my being and abilities, I felt like I was dropping down toward the center, both of myself and of the world at large. The colors, sights, and tastes of Africa—the morning sunlight, the faces of the people in the *bomas*, or small villages through which we trekked, all seemed somehow more familiar than exotic.

For days we trekked from *boma* to *boma,* up and down the parched hills of the African bush. We began each morning with a simple breakfast of tea, corn mush, eggs, and bread, and then started walking. As there wasn't much else to do other than take in the scenery, we spent a lot of time talking to the chief. His views of the world were absolutely fascinating. At one point he explained that the standard of wealth among his people was cattle. They raised a distinct breed that looked like a small Brahma bull. I assumed that because he was a chief, he must own many head of these livestock. When I asked him how many, however, the chief shrugged.

"I do not know," he said.

"You must have a rough idea."

The chief looked at me as if he couldn't comprehend the question.

"How could it be," I went on, "that cattle are the source of wealth and esteem within your tribe, and you, a chief, don't know how many you own?"

The chief thought for a few moments. "It is like this," he said. "When you go to a reunion of your family, do you count the number of persons present?"

"No," I told him.

"Still, if one of your relatives is missing from the gathering, you will know this, yes?"

I nodded. "Well," the chief said, "it is the same way with my cattle."

The *boma* residents emanated a similar wisdom and joy. These people had so little, in a material sense, and couldn't say what would happen to them tomorrow, and yet they were present, open, and connected to life in a way that most people in the West could only dream of. We are so removed from the kind of vitality they possessed that we don't even know it is missing.

As our group hiked in the terrific heat and dust, we continuously shed the expensive gear we had brought from home. We were all experienced in the outdoors and thought we'd packed only what was useful and essential, but each day in the bush taught us how much we could do without. We gave this extraneous stuff to the villagers, who were delighted by the gifts. Some of the people in the remote areas had never seen a single white man before, let alone our 10-man parade of white men, led by Tarzan and the Masai chief, our procession leaving a wake of high-tech Nike (which gave us some great gear to field-test) and REI gear along the way. All of this was merely the prelude to the real test that we had set out for ourselves. After days of conditioning ourselves to the bush, we were ready for the Ruaha.

We drove for more than 2 days to get to the jump-off point. We had now moved south, where it was hotter and more humid. This was not the Africa of my childhood fantasies. Like most of you probably did, I grew up watching Tarzan movies that depicted a thick, lush jungle teeming with wildlife. This was the dry season—the only time you can see much, and the season when all of the animals come to the water—and most everything was brown, dry, dusty, and parched. As we approached our starting point, we stopped in a village and picked up a game warden that the government wanted to send along. We thought this was curious, as we weren't hunting big game, but it was explained that this was for his safety, not ours or that of the animals. He and one other warden had the duty of protecting a preserve that was as big as the state of New Jersey, and all they were equipped with was a couple of rusty shotguns and a Land Rover that didn't run. This was their entire set of tools and weapons for contending with the scourge of poachers that were decimating the country. Thus it was determined that he would be safer going into the bush with all of us than on his own.

Prior to setting off, David and the warden conferred and then came to the group for a final briefing. "Before we head into the bush," he cautioned, "we need to be clear about a couple of things. The first is that once these Land Rovers leave, we are on our own. We are literally in the middle of nowhere, and there is no way to get help in here. What that means is that if anyone gets seriously hurt, you most likely won't make it out alive as we have no way to bring help. Even sending people ahead to the takeout point will do no good, as the Rovers won't be there until our appointed time in 10 days. The second thing we need to talk about is poachers. The warden says they are moving in this area, and we need to be clear about what is going to happen if we run across them."

We briefly discussed various options; most of us were in favor of leaving them alone, while the old EST trainers in the group wanted to "get them their lives back." Finally the game warden spoke up. He spoke softly but with some steel in his voice, and Tarzan translated. "We will kill them," he said. "What, do you think you are going to capture them and take them on your hike?" he asked. "They will kill you the first chance they get, and if we stumble across them and don't kill them first, then they will kill us." This was a sobering turn of events, which brought a stunned silence to the group. Tarzan then said, "If anyone wants to turn back, then now is the time." We looked at each other, and it was clear that no one was going to turn back—we had come too far.

We drove for another half day to our jump-off point, only to find that poachers had set the entire area on fire in the interval between the time Tarzan scouted it from the air and we got there. This was a tactic of the poachers: They would set big fires to drive the animals into areas where they could kill them. This seemed like a telling omen of what might lie ahead. I could see that some of the guys were nervous, but no one was going to back out now, so we strapped it up and set off.

We had embarked into one of the most remote parts of the planet, a place where extremely few white men had walked before, where the poachers shot to kill and burnt the bush to the ground to flush their illegal game. The earth still smoldered under a 2-inch carpet of ash. It seemed that the only life-forms that hadn't burnt were anything with thorns. This was no dreamy traipse among *bomas* where the natives welcomed us like long-lost relatives and treasured our cast-off windbreakers.

We walked through a severe and pitiless land. It was hot, it was humid, and the tsetse flies were a ravenous plague. They are like little horse flies, and their bites ripped out chunks of flesh and left angry welts. We doused DEET on our exposed skin, but that just seemed to sharpen the insects' appetite, so we eventually gave up. We walked in silence because we wanted to feel the land and avoid agitating the wildlife. This produced some amazing interactions with the animals, along with some seriously weird internal conversations.

"Well, you've really done it this time," I was thinking by the middle of the second day. "You've shelled out thousands of bucks for the privilege of participating in another Bataan death march."

The weather was insufferably hot and humid, the landscape looked like a thorn-ridden Mars, and our group was tired and cranky. Finally, just before dark on the second night, we broke out of the burn zone and into a sector of lush greenery. We made camp at a wide spot on the river and ate our first meal that wasn't covered in ash. After dinner we were in better spirits and dared each other to swim across the crocodile-infested expanse of water. Nobody ventured to get wet.

The next day was again hot, silent, and still. We were tired but our spirits had improved with the end of the burn, and we began the day with a sense of anticipation. We were so far out in the bush that oftentimes it seemed as if the animals didn't know enough to be afraid of humans. Gazelles would appear and walk alongside us for a while, and as long as we were silent and didn't make sudden movements, they would stay close and move with us.

We developed a routine: We would wake with the sun, walk until about noon, make a simple camp, have lunch, and then sleep for a few hours, as it was too hot to move during the middle of the day. We would then pack up and keep moving from about 3 p.m. until dusk, when we made camp for the night.

On the fourth day of the trek, following our breakfast, we packed up and began moving again as usual. A few hours into our journey, we walked around a big bend in the river and startled a pride of lions that were watering at the bank, perhaps 25 yards away. The animals reacted instinctively and with lightning speed. The adult lions tore upstream, concealing themselves in a patch of brush, while the cubs headed downstream and also disappeared into the bush. Tarzan, meanwhile, dropped his pack, lifted his rifle, and chambered a round, all the while backpedaling like a quarterback in order to achieve a clear line of fire.

He was not overreacting. The last place you want to be is between angry, protective lion parents and their cubs. That's right, just exactly where we were. The rest of us went into the routine we had been taught: Drop the pack off your back, swing it up in front so you have some protection, and stand ready. The trick with lions is not to run—if you do, they will come after you. This sounds simple enough in theory, but in the moment there was a growing gap between theory and practice. If you have been to the zoo or the circus, then you have heard a lion roar and you know what an impressive sound it is. But when you are 25 yards away from lions, there are no bars or trainers, and they are feigning charges at you, then the roars are personal: "Yeah, you! I am coming for you!" Believe me when I say it has a dramatically different effect on your body.

I'm not sure how long we stood there, frozen in that tableau at the bend of the river. It was probably only a few minutes, but time slowed down and every moment took on crystal clarity. As the seconds bled by, a new experience engulfed me. For years I'd been teaching centering, the practice of bringing mind and body together in the present moment. I thought I was good at it. I thought that I understood all of centering's nuances. But in that moment a new world opened up and I found myself in an unexplored new dimension of "center." There was no past, no future, just this infinite sense of now. The roars of those lions seemed to trigger some ancient biological memory: "Yes," I thought. "I have been here before." And in spite of this feeling of having already experienced this primal sensation, I also found myself reveling in a new emotion that was somewhere between joy and exhilaration but better, an emotion so fresh that I didn't have a word to describe it.

Finally Tarzan gestured for us to move toward the river so the adult lions could reunite with their cubs. This seemed like a good call. But as we neared the water, it erupted with a trumpeting bellow and a huge splash as an angry hippo let us know we had now trespassed into his territory, and he wasn't entertaining visitors today. *Holy shit*, I thought. *Three minutes ago I was slogging along, bored out of my mind, and now I'm in the middle of an Indiana Jones movie!*

Moving gingerly in single file along the riverbank, with the lions on one side of us and the hippo on the other, we were able to extricate ourselves without harm to anyone. That night, in camp, we discussed the incident. Some of my companions admitted feeling a bit of fear, while others reported feeling an adrenaline rush. I said that I'd experienced something unexpected and profound. Staring into the faces of those lions, hearing their roar, I had felt centered—present in the moment—in a way I'd never known before.

Nearly 20 years have passed since that exquisite moment on the bank of the Great Ruaha River, and yet I recall it often. The experience serves as a touchstone, a standard by which to gauge the power of living and moving from center.

You can attain authentic personal power only when your mind, body, and spirit are aligned. Because we want you to generate this kind of authentic personal power, we are going to build such an alignment in you. This alignment will produce a unity of thought and action that leads to greater competence, satisfaction, and contentment. We call this unity your "center," and the practice of developing and sustaining it is "centering." Over the course of decades of work with athletes, soldiers, and executives, I have invariably found that individuals who develop a capacity for centering display a stronger connection with themselves, with their family, and with their friends and community, and also experience a greater degree of satisfaction and fulfillment in everything they do.

The practice of centering derives from the Eastern traditions of martial arts and meditation. I came to it first through my practice of aikido, but centering really operates from the same principles in every tradition that uses this technique. You begin by aligning your body around its physical center, or *hara* (Japanese for "center" or "one-point"), which is located approximately a hand's span below the navel and equidistant between the front and back of your body. From this point, your center radiates outward to encompass all aspects of your life. Although I have just identified the center of your body, it isn't merely a thing, a physical place, or even a particular way of being; it is a living, dynamic process that increases our capacity for awareness, choice, accountability, action, integrity, and learning. Center is a state of wholeness in which effective action, emotional maturity, mental alertness, and spiritual connection function in harmony.

Centering produces unity of and in three realms. The first is the functional unity of the body, the second is unity of the mind, and the third is unity with the sacred, or unity of spirit. Each realm of centering, in turn, consists of three distinctions that enable the building of a practice: the qualities of being present, being open, and being connected.

CENTERING THE BODY

Let's talk a little bit about what "the functional unity of the body" means, and how you can begin to achieve it.

The process of becoming present, open, and connected in the body begins by focusing awareness on the somatic, or bodily, dimensions of length, width, and depth. All living things contain these three proportions: top to bottom, left to right, and front to back. Now I'm going to introduce you to the basics of how to align each of these three proportions.

To become present, you begin by centering along the dimension of length, which entails aligning the head, shoulders, hips, knees, and feet directly on top of one another. Once you've established an alignment along this vertical axis, you relax downward into the flow of gravity by releasing the tension in the forehead, eyes, jaw and chin, shoulders, abdomen, hips, pelvis, and legs. This lowers your center of gravity and transfers your weight from the muscles to the bones. When you let go of the muscular effort of holding yourself upright and allow your bones to support your body weight, you enter into a dynamic state of relaxation that increases your potential for efficient, powerful action.

Next you want to balance left to right along the horizontal axis, in order to center along the dimension of width. Because most of us are unilateral—either right-handed or left-handed—we unconsciously tilt to one side or the other. Balancing along the dimension of width, you stand with your weight equally distributed on both feet. This establishes symmetry between the left and right shoulders and both hip joints. The head is then situated directly over the chest.

Finally, you want to center along the dimension of depth. To do this, you align yourself front to back, balancing your body so it's tipped neither forward nor backward. Because humans are intensely future-oriented animals, with the majority of our sense organs located at the front of our bodies, we focus almost all our attention there and thus tend to "get ahead of ourselves." Preoccupied with our faces and fronts, with moving forward, we lose touch with our backs—and our history and traditions. By perpetually leaning forward into life, chasing survival or our interpretations of success, we often lose connection with the process of living in the moment. Aligning front to back, you will allow your spine to support you, which opens up your chest and heart.

The key to centering in all these realms and dimensions lies in focusing your attention on your *hara,* which, as we said earlier, lies about a hand's width below the navel and equidistant between front and back. In the Eastern martial-arts traditions this is called the "one-point," while in the West we recognize it as the physiological center of gravity. Shifting your attention from the din of thoughts to your body's center of gravity produces a sense of stability, strength, and groundedness. Although they may refer to it by a different name, dancers, running backs, bicyclists, actors, and other athletes and performers are all intimately acquainted with their *hara.* By bringing attention to center, you increase your capacity for alertness, calmness, and skillful action.

Let's now focus on the second part of centering the body: cultivating openness. In this case, "open" refers to the dilation of the senses and nervous system that occurs naturally when you relax and bring your attention fully to the bodily center. Openness provides a depth and texture to your range of experience. The easiest way to bring openness to yourself is with the breath. Each time you exhale, your body relaxes, and if you exhale with the intention of letting go of tension, of opening your nervous system to the world, then you will find that center begins to feel more like home. When you are present and open, life becomes more interesting and meaningful. To be present and open leads to being connected.

The quality of connection is at once simple and elusive. The internal connection of mind and body, for example, leads naturally to the connection of self to others. When present and open, you can experience relationships that are neither overly defensive nor excessively porous; you don't have to fret about "boundaries" or worry that you're either overwhelming another person or being overwhelmed yourself. Through center, you find a natural ease with the people around you, and from this foundation you branch out to connect to the world. Whether you live in the bustle of Manhattan or the open spaces of Colorado, you interact naturally with your environment. The centered individual moves through the world with a sense of peace and purpose.

Let's pause for a moment and talk about attention and awareness. Let me begin by giving you two organizing principles.

1. Control/choice follows awareness.
2. Energy follows attention.

These are both critical to understanding and learning the practice of centering, because the process of centering exposes the latent power inherent in your attention and awareness. Locating your center of physical gravity shows that you can consciously direct and organize your attention; instead of behaving like a weathervane whipped by the changing winds, your attention can serve you like a compass needle, always pointing to true north. By focusing your attention and expanding your awareness, you're able to shift your mood, listen to others with greater depth, increase your number of available choices, and move more powerfully in the world.

When you're aware of something, moreover, you increase the ways in which you can interact with it. *What you're unaware of will act upon you.* Until I become aware that the way I sit, stand, and walk puts stress on my lower back, for instance, I won't be able to change the way I sit and move. I will continue to suffer, unaware that I have the power to relieve the stress. If I merely direct my attention to my back, energy will begin to flow to that part of my body.

Attention can also flow in negative ways. When a woman directs her attention to her husband's snoring, for instance, his snoring seems to grow louder and more incessant. The truth is that the husband's snoring hasn't changed; it only seems that way to his wife, who is listening more intently for the grating sound. Focusing attention and energy on an unpleasant trait, trend, or incident only makes our experience more intense.

Training the attention, in short, is essential to the process of centering. Attention forms the glue of mind-body-spirit unity. Directing attention to the center opens the possibility of shifting from rigid, overly intellectualized thinking to a flow of more intuitive and skillful action. Becoming present, open, and connected increases your powers of perception. You grow more competent in your chosen work and gain confidence in yourself and your ability to move in the world.

The power of physical centering, however, comes with a caution: You can be seduced by this sense of physical strength and well-being, and forget that it is intended to be a foundation on which to build a bigger, more meaningful life. I'm sure we can all think of examples of famous athletes or performers who excel at their chosen sport or craft but otherwise live shallow and trivial lives. We cannot be content with merely centering and living in the body. We are multidimensional, and the body is the portal into the second realm of center, the mind.

CENTERING THE MIND

Some cultures believe that the mind is everything, that all physical reality is merely a manifestation of mental activity. In other traditions, the mind doesn't exist at all; it's merely a catchall invention of the Greeks, used to account for phenomena they couldn't otherwise explain. In our work on centering, we refer to the mind as the hub for the thinking and feeling processes.

The opening move in centering the mind consists of being alive in the present moment. Be here now. It means that as you read this sentence, you are not thinking about the film you saw last night or where you're going to go for lunch. To be present means to be fully in the moment; your mind does not wander off in time and space. This might sound simple, especially if you've never tried it, but achieving this presence of mind has formed the central mission of humanity's greatest sages. It requires vigilant training of your awareness and wholehearted engagement in the process of developing center.

Earlier, in the section on centering the body, I discussed the principles of attention, awareness, and energy. Now I'll introduce the essential "game" of centering. The point and challenge of the practice is to *realize when you're off center and to come back quickly*. No human being, not even the most advanced master of the martial arts, is centered all the time. That isn't possible, and it isn't the goal we have our sights set on. The point of the practice, and the purpose of training awareness, lies in developing the capacity to recognize when you stray off center, and—more importantly—how to return quickly.

Just as the smallest muscular contraction can take me off center in the physical realm, the most ephemeral passing thought can knock me off center in the mind. It can distract my attention from the present moment. As an ordinary human being, more-over, I am always thinking. More accurately, a succession of impressions constantly hurtles through my mind. As we mentioned earlier, the mind is like Grand Central Station, and thoughts and impressions are like trains crashing through, bound for unknown destinations. The uncentered passenger jumps on every train that comes by, regardless of how fast it's moving or where it's bound. The centered passenger, on the other hand, sits patiently on the platform, watching each train rumble by, waiting to embark on her intended trip.

The individual centered in her mind, in other words, has developed the capacity to stay present in the task, conversation, or reflection in which she's engaged. Because she is only human, however, she is perpetually tempted to chase after some unintended "train of thought." This is completely natural and inevitable. In fact, paradoxically, distraction forms the heart of the centering game: Realizing we're off center gives us the opportunity to get back on center quickly.

Indeed, straying off center becomes a problem only when you assess it as one, when you berate or otherwise punish yourself for following an errant train of thought. You could more profitably spend the energy you put toward blaming yourself into centering yourself. The challenge, the game, the trick, consists not of staying on center, but returning to center. The good news is that it is very easy to bring yourself back. It's like Dorothy in the Wizard of Oz. All you have to do is think about home—center. You don't need the ruby slippers or even have to click your heels three times. All you have to do is bring your attention back to your hara, your center, and you are back.

CENTERING THE SPIRIT

Ideally, as you spend time building your practice, you will develop to the point at which you consistently display increased self-confidence, growing strength of will and resolve, a capacity to learn and take new actions, and awareness of when you stray off center. You'll recognize that rather than a goal to be attained, centering is a permanent process in which you're continually engaged. Learn to relish the three-part game: getting knocked off center, noticing the situation, and quickly returning to center. Stand firm in your values, expressing and living them without righteousness or rigidity. Flexibility makes you stronger; your dignity can remain intact, even as you face the fires of life.

As you set out upon the never-ending, detour-filled journey toward achieving this competence, you will probably sense early on that the deeper power of centering originates from a source outside yourself. If you are honest and sincere, then you will eventually recognize the limitations of your will and awaken your desire for a connection to things beyond your capacity to create, a connection to the sacred and the realm of spirit. One of our current societal breakdowns is that we are rapidly losing sight of what distinguishes something as sacred. In our world, sacred can refer to anything from the smile on your child's face to the feeling of connection you have with your co-workers when you are really pulling together to complete a project. My call for centering the spirit is a call to expand your awareness of your existing connection with the deeper and more profound aspects of life.

The final element of centering, the alignment with the sacred, is built on the first two elements of centering the body and the mind. With this base you have the foundation from which you can step into the domain of centering the spirit.

When mind and body are present, open, and connected, we can most easily access the same distinctions of spirit. To be present, open, and connected in and to spirit is to be available to be touched by that which is both real and at the same time unexplainable. If we are not present and open in the body, then the connection to spirit may go unnoticed. Without the capacity to focus the awareness and the attention of the mind, life tends to simply happen around us. We become overwhelmed, and the notion of there being anything sacred vanishes in our constant rushing and reaching. We lose ourselves in scanning endless reports, checking plans, reading this and doing that. Centering the spirit affords us the luxury of a breath of time to see and feel that which is always there. In that moment, there exists the possibility of connecting to the sacredness of everyday life.

It seems that almost every adult in our modern world has come up against a moment when he suddenly looked around and wondered how he got here: this old, this settled in a life seemingly not of his design or choosing. This moment of insight often strikes at random, as you're obsessing over the numbers in the financial pages or watching your children play. *How did I get caught on this merry-go-round?* you might ask yourself. *When did I lose my wild, childlike spirit? This is not my beautiful life!* While this may sound—and feel—negative, even frightening, these are the moments that launch us on the path toward change.

Whatever causes this awakening, it triggers a shift in awareness and a new internal conversation. If you have been doing your practice, then your attention will drop down to the *hara* and radiate outward. In the domain of the spirit, center is more than the nexus point of your body; it is an orientation toward a universe beyond the scope of your mind and will. You find peace in the notion that we are a small part of an infinite mystery.

In this process of centering, you move out of an "I"-centered stance and open up to a broader wisdom and expression. In this alignment you are supported and nourished by that which operates without your assistance. It is that which is before language and time. It is a state beyond gender, age, experience, and knowledge. The person who is centered in this way is unperturbed by that which upsets others and at the same time demonstrates the capacity for decisive and spontaneous actions. Those who are centered in spirit affect others and the world through a presence that is altogether more expanded and powerful than the personality of a well-developed mind or body.

Groups, as well as individuals, can experience such moments. Just as centering produces personal power, a centered collective effort can lead to an empowered community, team, or business. We witness this when an underdog sports team taps a reservoir of collective energy and spirit to overcome seemingly insurmountable odds, or when groups from the military, business, and public-sector spheres coalesce to meet seemingly overwhelming challenges. Our entire nation, for instance, displayed an epic centering effort in responding to the crisis of 9/11.

Indeed, the process of centering lies at the heart of the human enterprise. As far as we can determine, we are the only living things simultaneously cursed and blessed with the knowledge that we're going to die. This knowledge both binds us to life and sets us apart from it. The process of centering allows us to build a unity of being, of body, mind, and spirit, that enables us to live creatively with this tension.

Centering also helps you negotiate the chaos and uncertainty of our era of unprecedented historical change. Humans have set these changes in motion, yet we feel increasingly helpless in the face of them. Centering will not eliminate the stress that can be associated with change, but it does empower you to respond to the chaos with authority, compassion, and grace. Centering supplies you with the ability to stop and reflect on your options and lets you move when others have jumped into panic-driven and unfocused action. The centered person finds his greatest satisfaction in service to something bigger than himself, as in the end that is the highest purpose of human beings. This could take any number of forms, from volunteering in your community to launching your own spiritual quest. Whatever path you take, the journey will have one consistent element.

Notice when you are off center and come back quickly. Come back, come back, and come back. This is centering; this is the dance that I practice each day, and that I witnessed so dramatically on that morning more than 20 years ago, in Africa, along the wild river, among the lions.

ASSIGNMENT #3

FOUR SECTIONS
TIME TO COMPLETE: 2 WEEKS, THEN THE REST OF YOUR LIFE

We are about to open a new world for you, and that world moves from center. Centering is a lifelong practice, and my promise is that if you start today, then you will find that in a very short amount of time you will start to experience yourself and your world in an entirely new way.

SECTION #1

Let's start with the basic step of getting you centered in your body. For the first step of this process you will need a partner, so even if you aren't working with a team, ask someone to assist you for a few minutes. It won't take long, and he or she may have some fun in the process.

Stand with your feet about shoulder-width apart, and keep them planted while you move around a bit and just get a sense for how your body feels. When you are in touch with how you are feeling both physically and emotionally, bring the movement to a stop and direct your attention to your head. What you want to do is be sure that your head is on straight on top of your shoulders. It shouldn't be cocked to one side or inclined forward or back. You chin is level. Your eyes stay open, the muscles around them relaxed. Your forehead and neck are relaxed, as is your jaw, which you can do by simply parting your lips so your teeth aren't touching. Your partner will be helpful here, as oftentimes what you think is straight or level may not be. Throughout the process be sure that you continue to breathe. Holding your breath is common when moving into new territory, but it's the last thing you want to do while learning to center.

Now we bring your attention to your shoulders. Start by rolling them in a big circle and then letting them relax. Imagine your favorite shirt or blouse draped on its hanger in your closet, and strive to relax your shoulders into this same shape. The shoulders are not up and rigid, nor are they collapsed downward. They are square and relaxed.

Next we go to your hips. You want to be sure that your weight is distributed evenly and that you aren't leaning on one side more than the other. You aren't twisted in any way, and your shoulders and core sit squarely above your hips.

Now let's move to your knees. You want your knees to be flexed or unlocked. Most people stand with their knees locked, and not only is this hard on the joints, but it also produces a rigidity in the rest of the body. To unlock your knees, don't bend them; just unlock them. This will enable you to really feel your feet and their connection to the ground.

Finally we get to the last and most critical piece. I will let you know in advance that this is going to sound and look a bit strange, so I don't recommend you go around in public doing this. Lay one of your palms flat against your belly. Touch your thumb to your belly button and then tap your little finger against your belly a few times. Your little finger should be a hand's span below your thumb. This is where your center point, or "hara," is located on your body. As you are tapping your little finger, imagine that with each tap a laser beam is moving through you, from the point that your little finger is tapping to your back. Halfway along that line is the exact center of your body. In the physical realm, this is your center of gravity. For our purposes, it is your center.

To complete this first phase, I want you to begin to use your breath. Imagine as you inhale that your lungs reach all the way down into your pelvis, so that as you take an "in" breath, you are breathing all the way down into your center and the pelvic region. As you exhale, imagine that you are breathing out any tension or stress that you don't need.

Now we get to the part where a partner is necessary. So far it all sounds simple, and you should notice that you feel a bit more relaxed and present than normal as you work through these early steps. It is, however, too easy to delude yourself, so we have a little centering test.

Have your partner stand off to one side of you so that he or she is facing your shoulder. Have him or her put one hand just behind you, not touching but close by. Now undo all of what we just did and go in the opposite direction. Make yourself tense and uptight. Raise your shoulders, tighten your jaw, let your breath become fast and shallow, clench your cheeks together (your lower cheeks, that is), lock your knees, and tighten all of the muscles in your legs. This is in essence the opposite of center, and what I want to give you is a comparison between the two states. The test is simple. Have your partner make contact with your chest, just above the breastbone, using the little finger edge of his or her hand. Once contact is established, he or she will gradually put pressure on you through his or her hand. Your job is to keep your feet planted in one place—do not move them—and see how much pressure it takes for you to lose your balance and start to fall backward. I don't want you to fall down. When you begin to feel yourself falling, catch yourself by moving your feet. Do this a few times so you have some baseline data on how much force it takes to move you.

SECTION #2

Now your partner is going to position him- or herself exactly as before and conduct the exact same test. This time, though, you are going to center yourself first. Check that you're aligned on all three planes, that your head is right above your relaxed shoulders, that your hips are balanced, your knees unlocked, your weight evenly distributed on both feet, and that your breathing is deep, centered in your belly, and regular. Bring your palm to your belly and tap your little finger on your center point. When you are ready, have your partner test you again. Now pay attention, as there are a few beginner's mistakes you want to avoid. The first is that you may want to lean forward to meet your partner's hand as it is coming toward you. This is normal, but it takes you off center—so don't do it. Next, your shoulders may come up when your partner makes contact with you. Let them relax. Remember our adage that energy follows attention, and don't let your attention become drawn to your partner's hand. Instead, keep your attention on your center. Tapping the little finger helps, as does imagining that what your partner is doing is sending energy in through your chest and down to your center.

When you are ready, have your partner test you. What you should notice is that you are much harder to move off center. Being centered doesn't alter the laws of physics, so at some point you will topple over. It should, however, take considerably more effort than when you are tensed. If you find that it isn't working, then pay attention to your feet and knees, as you are most likely keeping your attention and energy on your partner's hand. If you find yourself bending, Gumby-like, at the waist, then you want to put a bit more steel into your spine, as centering is a dynamic and powerful way of being in the world. This isn't about collapsing when life comes at you.

If you continue to have trouble feeling any difference, then go to *The Power to Transform* Web site at www.thepowertotransform. net. There you will see some video clips on centering that are designed to help you through the beginner stage.

Believe it or not, that is the essence of the practice. The game, again, is to develop your awareness so that you notice when you are off, and build your capacity to bring yourself back to center. Everything we are going to do is designed to sharpen your awareness and hone your skill at getting back to center.

SECTION #3

One of the adages I gave you earlier in this chapter was that *control/choice follows awareness*. Now that you know the basic distinction of being on and off center, we are going to work on expanding your awareness. This part of the assignment is simple. I want you to get a pad of little Post-It notes and invent some symbol for yourself that stands for centering. It could be a simple C or any sort of visual reminder that you like. Make 5 to 10 copies of this reminder and put them in places where you will see them regularly. The minimum requirement is one on your bathroom mirror, one on the refrigerator, one on your computer screen, one on the rearview mirror of your car, and one on whatever you carry around as a day planner, PDA, iPhone, or other device that you use on a daily basis. You can then put a few more around your home or workplace, wherever you will run across them with some regularity. For the next 2 weeks, I want you to keep these reminders up, and each and every time you see one of them, use it as a trigger to get you to center. Remember that all it takes is a split second to bring your attention to your center. Beware of your enemies of learning, as your internal cynic will try and tell you that you are too busy, this won't work, you can't do this because it is too dorky. Don't fall for these distractions. Focus on your commitment to learn and just do the practice. It takes no time and next to no effort.

After the first week, take a few minutes and make some written notes on what you are observing about yourself now that you have begun to develop a centering practice. In particular, see if you can notice a pattern in the things that knock you off center. Pay attention to what you are doing to bring yourself back to center and make notes about both of these. If you are working with a partner, share your notes. If not, keep them for your reference.

Continue the practice for a second week and repeat the process of making notes. Again, beware of the enemies of learning. Now they will try and convince you that you've got it down already and don't need the reminders. Don't fall for it. Stay committed to maintaining your practice. When you have completed the second week and the notes that go with it, you are ready for the next stage.

SECTION #4

I am now going to introduce you to a simple process we call the two-step. This is a simple physical practice that, while easy to learn, is not so easy to teach with only verbal descriptions. Therefore, for this part of the assignment, you need to go to the Web site, where you will find, under the "Chapter 5—Centering" button, a video demo of the two-step. Watch the video and get the practice down.

Once you have the basics, the rest is practice: That is the key to everything. For this particular practice, do 10 two-steps in the morning before work, 5 at some point during the day, and 10 anytime after work. The challenge will be to "mind your mind" as you do this. This is a more advanced form of learning to be centered. There is no point doing the two-step if your assess-o-matic mind is running full speed. That is just another form of being off center. You are going through the motions, but your mind is not present. Do the practice with your mind focusing on the movement, deepening your awareness of your body as you do it. Feel your breath, feel your feet, feel your arms. What do you notice about your center of gravity? Make some notes on your practice after the first few days, and pay attention to what your mind is doing. Again, if you have a partner, share your notes about what you are seeing in your practice. If not, keep them for reference.

Keep up the daily repetitions of the two-step. You may as well get used to this, as you will be doing it for a while. Don't listen to your inner cynic if she tries to convince you that this isn't important so you can skip it, that you are too busy, or that you're a special case that doesn't need to do it. If you find that conversation creeping into your awareness, then that is evidence that you should probably do more. Keep the reps up and have a conversation with your partner, and make some notes regarding what you are beginning to observe about the quality of your two-steps.

- Are you getting any better?
- How do you know?
- How do they feel?
- What is your mind doing while you do the practice?

You will get better just by doing the practice regardless of what your mind says about it, but it will be a stronger practice if you can work your mind into the practice as opposed to having to contend with it to get the practice done. Do this practice for at least 3 weeks, then make some notes on what you see has shifted in your way of moving in the world. When you have completed your notes, keep returning to the practice and keep it up for 6 months. Yes, every day for 6 months! Then make a second set of notes that touch on the same points that you did with the first. In particular notice what your mind dishes up as excuses to not do the practice. When you have completed your second set of notes, return to the practice and continue your two-steps for the rest of your life. Yes, I am serious—the rest of your life.

You are now equipped with all that you need to build a lifelong centering practice. Yes, there is more to it, as well as lots of additional moves and practices you can learn, but you now know the basics, and they will be sufficient if you commit to doing the work. More importantly, you know the game. Notice when you are off center and come back quickly. In the end, that's all there is to know.

Remember, *control/choice follows awareness*, and *energy follows attention*. For some final words of wisdom, I leave you with an old Samurai adage that we use in our live courses. *Expect nothing—be ready for anything.*

———————————

SIX

CULTIVATING AWARENESS

THE RANGE OF WHAT WE THINK AND DO
IS LIMITED BY WHAT WE FAIL TO NOTICE.
AND BECAUSE WE FAIL TO NOTICE WHAT WE
FAIL TO NOTICE THERE IS LITTLE WE CAN DO
TO CHANGE UNTIL WE NOTICE HOW FAILING TO
NOTICE SHAPES OUR THOUGHTS AND DEEDS.

—R.D. LAING

The first section of this book set the foundation for the challenging and exciting work of transforming you and reshaping your future. I introduced the concept that language is generative. We use it not only to describe reality, but also and more importantly, to create it. We have the power to change our lives by changing not only our actions, but also the stories that we tell about ourselves and others. You saw that one of the fundamental tools for change is developing competence in the basic linguistic moves. You also saw that transformation can occur only via authentic learning, and that authentic learning requires practice, patience, and perseverance. You can reconfigure yourself and along the way you will develop *somatic transformation, social mastery, and spiritual strength*. Once you let go of the notion that there is some magic pill that could grant you instant change and make the commitment to authentic learning, the door to a new future opens. Blocking the doorway to your new future are the enemies of learning. You have already confronted some of them, and they will be back for a return visit. That you are still engaged in the process of shaping a new you tells me that you are committed to your transformation and serious about having a new life. Congratulations!

In the foundation chapters, I also introduced you to the power of centering: living your life and moving in the world from your center, the somatic state of being present, open, and connected. I showed you that as you build your centering practice, you will learn to move through the world with consistent presence, purpose, and power.

Over the past 25 years, in my work with athletes, soldiers, and corporate leaders, I have discovered that these performers have much in common. They may use different vocabularies according to their respective professions, but they all operate according to a very specific set of shared convictions, which we have distilled into a set of principles and declarations that we call the Universal Performance Principles. No matter what your work, your nationality, or your organizational affiliation, living your life by these principles will help you to change in the ways that you want to change and earn you membership in the global collective of authentic learners who are working to reshape the world.

Cultivating awareness is the first step toward shaping a new you. In order to change yourself, you must first be able to see yourself. Developing awareness means becoming a more competent observer of yourself and your world. You must develop the capacity to observe your body, your emotions, and your internal and external conversations. How do my conversations create my reality? How do the ways that I carry and care for my body determine my experience of myself and my life? How do my moods and emotions shape my world?

Once you begin asking these questions and honestly assessing the answers, you will almost certainly notice a gap between the actions you take and the internal vision or story that you've created about yourself. You will also notice that all of the dramatic, tedious, and exciting scenes in your life story share one common character: namely, you. That same you also happens to be the only character in the story whose role you can change. To affect change, you must begin with a deeper, more honest awareness of yourself and how you operate in the world.

This new awareness works on both your interior and exterior dimensions. The challenge is to extend your range of perceptions. In the realm of the senses, what new things can I see, taste, smell, hear, and touch? How do I recognize the subtle signs that I am off center? In the realm of the self, how can I more deeply experience my unique way of being human? Beyond the level of personality, how can I expand the boundaries of my awareness at every level?

When I operate with a low level of awareness, the number of options available to me is reduced. I simply cannot see many choices, and thus the only course of action that seems viable is the one that I follow by habit—the same blind habits that have produced the limited results that are currently making me feel stuck.

Let me give you an example of what I am pointing to. In the first chapter of the book, I told you about my experience of delivering a briefing at Fort Hood. Now I want to take you a bit deeper into the background that led us to that presentation. As you may recall, in the early days HP2 worked exclusively with athletes and generated powerful results with individual performers and teams. But the bulk of our clients were amateurs, and thus while we were doing very good work and making a big difference with these individuals, we weren't exactly raking in the money. This was in the days before Nike, Adidas, and Reebok invested heavily in athletes and their development, so in those days we were used to living on very tight budgets.

Our success with athletes caught the attention of the Army, and in short order we found ourselves at Fort Hood, Texas, where the commander had a mandate to explore new ways to train and develop soldiers. In our initial meeting, the colonel in charge of the exploratory group detailed the series of problems that the Army faced. There were too many sick calls, too many soldiers who were overweight, too many who couldn't pass the physical-fitness test, and drug and alcohol problems. He went on to detail the regime of remedial programs they had set up to deal with all of this, and asked that we bring our talents to bear in particular on the problem of the soldiers who couldn't pass the physical-fitness test.

We explained to the room of assembled brass that all of their problems were related, and that we could take care of the lot of them at the same time. This got their attention, and we went on, in general terms, to explain how we would do it. The officers were intrigued and asked how much it would cost. I explained that this was not some packaged program that we were selling them. What we had done was lay out a generic framework for a holistic solution. "That's nice, but how much is it going to cost?" the colonel repeated. When I informed him that I didn't have a figure ready, he suggested that we all take a lunch break, during which I should work out a budget to present to the group after we ate.

Off we went to the local Sizzler, where I pulled out my legal pad and set to work crafting a budget. The dilemma was that we had never done business with the government before, and therefore I had no idea what it was going to take to accomplish many of our goals. As a buffer, I put together some pretty big numbers, and when I totaled it up we were looking at a figure of some $95,000 for the design and delivery of our test program. With a bit of a gulp, I took our new budget back for the afternoon meeting. Once there, I wrote it all out on a flip chart, then went through the numbers for the colonels and other officers in the room. As I was getting to the bottom line, I noticed that the room became increasingly quiet. When I finished, the colonel in charge turned to the colonel next to him and said, "Well, Colonel, what do you think?" I could tell he was thinking about how to frame his answer, and I was getting a bit nervous. He finally said, "Frankly, sir, I would rather not say in front of them." At this point, my savage inner critic had a field day. *Nice job, greed head. You had to put all those big numbers in there just to play it safe, and now look at what you did. You scared them off!* The colonel in charge persisted, insisting that his fellow colonel give him an honest response. "Well, frankly, sir," he said at last, "we can fire up the armor assigned to the test unit in question and let it idle for 15 minutes and burn $95,000. That's nothing!" The colonel in charge turned to me as he said, "Now I want to be clear that we are expecting a top-tier program here. Are you guys sure you thought of everything?"

This was a very big lesson in awareness. I had been operating at my historical level of awareness, shaped by and limited to our work with largely amateur athletes. I was completely blind to the world of the Army, with its radically different scale. Thus I got a big wake-up call. In this case I was fortunate, as the wake-up wasn't too painful and opened a new world to us.

As you expand your awareness, you will be able to recognize new possibilities. You'll feel more at peace with life, more confident and ambitious, and you will be more likely to be regarded by others as alert, vital, and optimistic. To achieve this state, you must cultivate the capacity to observe yourself in both the interior and exterior dimensions, to "see" both yourself and your world clearly.

Honing this vision requires the conscious discipline of "involved observing," the ability to simultaneously take action and observe yourself in action. You become a scientist whose field of study is yourself. You observe how you operate in various situations; you determine what sort of conversations and events trigger specific reactions and responses. The central challenge is to see yourself as you operate in cooperation and coordination with other people. It is learning to listen to your internal discourse about life, work, yourself, and your relationships, and remembering that it is all just your way of seeing and assessing the world, not the truth.

The vast majority of people don't have practices for expanding their awareness and are left to observe themselves through the distorted prism of the inner conversations and the harsh eye of their savage inner critics. Thus they are frequently mystified when others "misinterpret" their actions.

Cultivating such awareness is a lifelong journey that begins with the simple declaration, "I choose to be more aware." Here are some orienting points to remember as you begin.

- Each human being has inside him- or herself, a chorus of little voices. We refer to this phenomenon as your inner congress. This is part of being human and doesn't mean you are crazy. We will focus our attention on one of these voices that we have dubbed your inner critic. If you are reading this and asking, "What voices?" this is the very phenomenon I am talking about.

- Each human being also has what we call an "observer." This is the aspect of your self that can watch and "observe" all of the chattering that your "inner congress" engages in. It is your observer that decides which of the voices you pay attention to. Much of our work will focus on teaching you how to design and shape the observer that you are so that you make more powerful choices.

- To expand your external awareness, you must practice observing the world. To observe carefully means to expand your set of distinctions about the world.

- You can be aware of others only to the degree that you're aware of yourself.

- Self-awareness is not the same as self-centeredness. When I'm aware of myself, I am more in touch with everything and everyone around me. I am more open, available, sensitive, and awake.

- Awareness requires being fully present in the here and now.

Our work on awareness is intended to deepen your capacity to see yourself. There are three aspects of you in particular that I want to focus your awareness on. The first is the nature of your mind. It is essential that you understand the fundamental nature of your mind, as, like it or not, it is currently running you. Philosophers, scientists, and clerics of all sorts have spent hundreds of years debating the big question, "What is the mind?" I am not going to weigh in on that discussion, as resolving this grand dilemma isn't likely to make any difference as we work to shape a new you. Instead of a philosophical approach, let's take a much more practical, or operational, view.

For the sake of clarity and simplicity, let's hold that *your mind is a highly evolved, highly effective, pattern-recognition device.* Human beings have been evolving on planet Earth for 4 to 5 million years. This has provided ample opportunity for the mind to develop a highly refined capacity to recognize and remember patterns. Only during the last 10,000 to 15,000 years have people been "civilized," and the last century alone has witnessed most of the technological revolution. What this means is that for 99.9 percent of our evolutionary process, we lived in what we'd now term "primitive" conditions. It was during that vast period of time that we developed the pattern recognition capabilities that still drive us today.

In primitive days, a hunting party would set out to provide food for the whole community. Let's imagine that a group of these hunters happened across a saber-toothed tiger, a creature they had never seen before. The beast looked interesting, so one of the early humans guilelessly approached it—and paid for his curiosity by becoming the tiger's lunch. Imprinting this new informational pattern in their minds (big cat with big front teeth = I'm lunch), the rest of the group ran away, to resume the hunt another day.

On the next expedition, two kinds of hunters set out, those whose pattern-recognition device was efficiently functioning, and those for whom pattern recognition remained a work in progress. When the former group of hunters spotted a big cat that shared certain characteristics with the saber-toothed tiger they'd encountered on the last hunt and therefore fit the same pattern, they recognized the pattern and either avoided or killed the beast. The second group was again wondering what the creature was, again approached it naively, and met with an unfortunate end. This group was quickly weeded out of the human gene pool, for obvious reasons.

An oversimplification? Of course. But the point is that we've been evolving our pattern-recognition skills for millions of years. In this regard, humans around the world are all exactly the same. From the Wall Street bond trader to the Kalahari bushman, our minds have evolved to enable a vast capacity for rapid pattern imprinting and recognition. The good news is that this is a survival instinct that has served us well.

The rest of the news is that in addition to being a highly evolved, highly effective pattern-recognition device, the mind is extremely lazy, highly resistant to change, and deeply committed to being right and playing it safe.

While the desire to play it safe has proven a highly effective survival mechanism on a basic level—going back to our days as prey of the saber-toothed tiger, we know instinctively to flee in the face of apparent danger—the problem is, we don't live a hunting-and-gathering existence any longer. Playing it safe often fails us in a fast-paced world where the only constant is change. In today's world, our lives are rarely in danger and our livelihoods depend on authentic, lifelong learning, which, as we've seen, entails continually pushing beyond our comfort zone. So we need to learn a response other than fight or flight when we face challenges and confront our fears.

There is a strong connection between your mind's laziness and its commitment to being right. Once your mind lays down a given pattern, it is very reluctant to alter that pattern. Again, in the fight-or-flight survival mode, this tendency makes perfect sense: It wouldn't work to have to rethink whether the tiger was really dangerous every time you crossed paths with one. Once a pattern is fixed in place, the mind tends to go for a quick reference rather than making a full and new examination.

This tendency gets us in trouble when we come across something or someone new. In those moments, your mind does what it does, survival-based pattern recognition, and as it is lazy, it tends to look for what we call a *previous similar*. It very quickly does a memory-file search for a pattern based on a similar person, thing, situation, or idea that you encountered previously. When your mind finds one that is close, or more often one that is somewhat close, it can put the new phenomenon into a pre-existing "box" and relax. It doesn't have to expend the energy and effort to truly explore what is new. The mind's tendency is to be lazy, so it shoehorns the new into a ready-made box, thus draining the new thing of both its threat and its possibility.

Here are two potent examples of how placing new things into pre-existing categories can get you in trouble:

When you first happened to see this book in a store, your attention may have been grabbed by the title or the cover, and you picked it up. Part of you was curious, but your mind kicked in and the internal conversation likely sounded like this: "Another book devoted to developing my potential; I read a few of these already and nothing changed. This is just like the others, so the outcome won't be any different. Why should I bother?"

Let's take a work-related example. There is a new account manager in your office. His name is Phil. He is tall, brown-haired, and left-handed. Your mind quickly goes to work. "He reminds me of Alex. Alex is a tall, brown-haired, left-handed account manager, and he's a jerk. Phil's probably a jerk too."

In the first instance, instead of taking the trouble to read the new book about developing your potential, you assume you already know everything there is to know on the subject based upon other, different books you've read in the past, and therefore you miss out on the chance to shape a new you.

In the second instance, instead of getting to know Phil, you let your mind merely draw upon the memory of some guy he vaguely resembles, and whom you didn't care for, and therefore you miss out on the chance to meet a potentially great person.

Drawing upon the previous similarity robs you of the possibility for growth: The book might change your life; Phil might become your best friend.

Now that you understand your mind's process of rapid pattern recognition and response—we call this process the *conditioned response*—I want you to focus your awareness on noticing when you do this. The conditioned response is the instant, semi-conscious assessment and automatic reaction to the people you meet and the events that occur on a daily basis. This deeply ingrained evolution-ary adaptation works against you as you move to expand your awareness.

Here is an example. Imagine yourself in a forest campground at dusk. You walk around the side of your tent and see a snake on the ground. For most of human history, encounters with snakes haven't worked out well, so we have developed a conditioned response when we meet one. Instead of taking a scientific approach ("Hmmm, looks like a snake, but I'm not sure. I better step up close to see if it really is a snake and, if so, what kind"), the mind defaults to the survival-based conditioned response—*Snake! Run!*—and your body springs into action.

You may not actually run, but at the very least you'll come to an abrupt halt and jump away from the snake. Your mind will short-circuit the normal inquiry process and default into survival mode. This all happens in an instant and is a very well-honed survival mechanism.

So what's the problem with this scene? Nothing, until you take a second look and realize that the snake your conditioned response reacted to was really a piece of rope that one of your kids had dropped. In which case you hope no one witnessed your mini freak-out, and that you haven't seriously compromised your cool.

"What's the big deal? Better safe than sorry," you say. In the case of the wilderness, I won't argue with you. Unless you want to become a safari guide, it's probably not a big deal if you freak out when you encounter wild animals—or coiled ropes that look like snakes. But in daily life, these conditioned responses can pose a host of problems.

At the physical level, the most obvious is the stress response triggered by the sympathetic nervous system's reaction to the con-ditioned response. When I am faced with any of life's daily chal-lenges, a past-due deadline at work, a child throwing a tantrum, or being cut off in traffic, my conditioned response is to go into a lesser version of the same survival mode that the saber-toothed tiger produced. Adrenaline kicks in, my heart rate rockets, my breathing turns shallow, my nostrils flare, and my palms sweat. Sound familiar?

The prehistoric hunter faced the saber-toothed tiger only on rare occasions. The vast majority of his life was much more passive, pastoral, and predictable. His stress response passed, his emotions recovered, and his physical systems returned to baseline or normal, where they would stay steady for days or weeks on end. But in our contemporary lives, we rarely resolve stressful moments in a rapid, decisive manner, and they occur on a daily basis as opposed to occasionally. As a result, we experience the stress response too often, its effects linger, and over time this can produce serious health problems.

Let's look in a different realm, one we have all been through: the disagreement with a loved one. You and your husband/wife get into a fight. At some point during the argument, he or she says something nasty with a particular tone of voice. Your feelings are hurt, and it takes a while to recover from this verbal assault. A few months later, you are engaged in a conversation with your partner, and he or she falls into that same hurtful tone of voice that characterized the previous disagreement. Your mind goes into a conditioned response, and your defenses immediately go up to stave off what is certain to be the same sort of assault you experienced last time. You bristle and raise your own voice. You are clearly off center, certainly no longer in the moment, and no longer listening to what your partner is saying. Your conditioned response has taken over.

Now remember: *Your mind is a highly evolved, highly effective pattern-recognition device.* It is also extremely lazy, very resistant to change, and deeply committed to being right and playing it safe. It tends to operate on a series of what we call *conditioned responses*, as they are an effective survival mechanism. Unfortunately, while conditioned responses serve hunters well, they severely limit our ability to expand our awareness in the modern world.

This brings us to the next point that I want to focus your awareness on, and that is your mind's capacity for making and honing distinctions. This is a skill that we want to cultivate. Your mind isn't going to want to do this, as it requires effort, but it is critical for your capacity to create a new you.

To distinguish a thing is to isolate it from the background in which it exists or to separate one thing from another. It is the capacity to discern, and the discerning mind is what we seek to cultivate.

Here is a simple visual example. You are taking a walk with a friend, and she says, "Look at that cute little squirrel on that oak tree over there." You look at the oak tree but can't see the squirrel, which is camouflaged by the tree's branches and leaves.

"Where is it?" you ask your friend. "I don't see it."

Your friend carefully explains where to look, but you still can't see the squirrel. You're beginning to feel a bit embarrassed when finally the squirrel moves, your eyes pick up the motion, and suddenly you can distinguish the squirrel from the background of the tree.

The same process occurs when making distinctions in other aspects of life. As we mature, we naturally, by virtue of a wider range of experience, begin to build a bigger set of distinctions. We learn about the subtleties and nuances of life. We learn what works and what doesn't. We find where our passions lie and pursue them, and in so doing build a richer and deeper set of distinctions. These enable us to be more powerful players in the game of life. Our goal in our work together is to build you a much more powerful set of distinctions about you, your potential, and how to realize it.

As you've progressed in your career, for instance, you have likely developed a set of distinctions and moves unavailable to those outside of your trade or profession. A surgical nurse, for example, accrues a wide set of distinctions regarding surgical instruments. She can distinguish between a scalpel, forceps, and a retractor, and among sizes and other specifics of each class of instrument. You and I would look at the same set of instruments and see only a daunting collection of sharp, silver objects seemingly designed for some gruesome torture.

Or consider your local mechanic and his refined set of distinctions concerning automotive functions. You take your car to him reporting that, "The engine is making a funny clicking sound and feels like it's running rough." This basic level of distinction is the best you can manage concerning the subject, while your mechanic, by contrast, turns on the ignition, listens for 20 seconds, and says, "You have a stuck lifter, and the roughness is due to the engine running too rich, which is causing it to flood out slightly when you accelerate."

Your mechanic's distinctions provide him with a set of moves for working on your car, moves that are unavailable to you, just as your primary physician's set of distinctions enable her to tend to your physical health in a manner unavailable to you. Every craft, trade, and profession possesses a singular set of distinctions. In order to act competently and powerfully in a given vocation, you must first learn its distinctions.

Distinctions also operate on the personal and interpersonal levels. Suppose, for instance, that you and your boyfriend have a fight. It seems as if you and he are butting heads all the time lately. You have coffee with a friend, and she asks how your relationship is going. "Oh, it's a mess," you reply. "All we do is fight, and I have no idea what to do about it." Driven by this encompassing assessment, a sense of despair settles in. Eventually, you take the only course of action that seems available: You end the relationship. You subsequently go through a period of "healing," during which you convince yourself that you've learned some valuable lessons from the recent, ill-fated affair. When you embark on a new relationship, however, the same dark dynamic emerges. Because you haven't developed a useful set of distinctions in this realm, you are left with few options to deal with the inevitable difficulties that arise in relationships. Again, you and your new boyfriend seem to fight all the time. Again, you break up. Are we on familiar ground?

Let's see what happens if we look at the same set of circumstances through a richer set of distinctions about relationships. I can provide you with an entire book's worth of material on relationships, but this one isn't focused on improving your love life. However, personal relationships are an important part of any human life. The new you that you are shaping—the you that is capable of change—will be able to bring your powers of observation and centering to your personal relationships as well as your professional ones.

For the sake of simplicity, let me suggest that under the big banner of "relationship," there is a dynamic subset of arenas of action, distinctions of behavior, and practices that can either bring people together or apart, qualities by which people define themselves and rate their success or happiness within their relationships. This list includes public identity, money, spirituality, sexuality, career, domestic chores, parenting, hobbies, and a few more items that we can attend to later. If you were to assess how satisfied you are in each domain of your relationship and grade it on a scale of 1 to 10, then you might reveal something interesting and freeing. Let's say you give yourself an 8 on public identity (people think you are a great couple), a 3 on money, an 8 on spirituality, an 8 on career, a 7 for hobbies, and a 9 on sex. All in all, these are very good marks. However, if you don't have the awareness to distinguish each of these separate domains and hold them as separate, what tends to happen is that you let all of the good collapse into the bad. We refer to this tendency as collapsing and catastrophising. The reality is that while you might fight exclusively about money, everything else in your relationship is working. If you have the capacity to make these distinctions, then you can see a host of possible actions that aren't available to you otherwise. Without being able to make these distinctions, it's possible that you could still fall into the story: "My relationship is on the rocks; all we do is fight." This is what we term a global assessment (always ungroundable), and as you will recall, human beings act out of these assessments. The failure to make distinctions—about relationships and other things—is frequently a source of trouble.

If you are serious about growing up and being in an adult relationship, then you must train yourself to make distinctions and develop a more supple and powerful stance in dealing with your partner. Throughout the remainder of the book, I will continue to push you to use your awareness to refine a broader set of distinctions about you and your life, as this capacity is critical to expanding you and your world.

Now I want to keep my promise to show you ways to quiet your inner cynic, that nasty little voice that is constantly yammering in your head. One of the wonders of being a human being is that we all come equipped with an inner observer. This is the little voice in your mind that offers you a running commentary on every thought and action. It's like a backseat driver constantly telling you that every turn you make is wrong. The cynical tone of the inner voice arises from a conditioned response: the natural desire to avoid pain. The pain in question is more often emotional than physical. It typically originates from a negative experience in the past. You trusted someone and got burned; you flunked your first math test; your first girlfriend broke your heart; your first boss was a tyrant; you attended a motivational seminar and your life failed to change.

Whatever the details of the experience, you trusted once and believe you were betrayed. Your mind seeks to avoid repeating the emotional pain associated with that betrayal. You were disappointed, embarrassed, humiliated, or ashamed, and rather than risk suffering those emotions again, your inner voice learned to respond to a new situation with cynicism, which is a conditioned response.

"You tried that once and look what happened," the savage critic whispers. "You were exposed and humiliated; you looked like a fool. This situation is just like that other one. Do you want to go through that torture again? Don't take another risk. Play it safe. Keep your head down. Don't get fooled again."

The cynical little voice makes a strong argument for playing it safe, and in so doing works against expanding your awareness. Indeed, the voice has often been irresistible. Now you have a new way of working with it, and that will be our jumping-off point for your next assignment.

ASSIGNMENT #4

FOUR SECTIONS
TIME TO COMPLETE: 1 MONTH

SECTION #1

The first part of this assignment is simple. Let's check in and see how you are doing at battling the enemies of learning. This is a good chance to expand your awareness, so take a few minutes and write some notes about what you are now observing about the way the enemies of learning show up. This is important, because I don't want you to think that, just because we worked on this once, you are done with it. Remember our adage—control follows awareness. You will never get control of the enemies of learning if you aren't honing your awareness of how they influence you. Which of them seems to be pulling at you? What circumstances seem to bring them on? Have you found that one or two have faded, only to be replaced by some new ones? For example, you may notice that by virtue of all of the work we have done on learning, you are no longer looking for the magic pill of instant learning. That is great. But stay alert and see if the fading desire for the magic pill has been replaced by constant assessing or some new characterization: "I can't do this, I'm too busy, old, young, whatever." If you are really aware, then you will begin to notice that eventually all of them will pay you a visit. Just as the game of centering requires you to notice when your attention flutters away and return back to center, again and again, you should also train yourself to notice when the enemies of learning show up, so that you can recognize them, send them away, and continue the vital work of shaping a new you. Your challenge is to simply see them for what they are: fear-based attempts by your mind to avoid the work of expanding your awareness of yourself and your world. If you are working with a partner or team, set aside some time to compare notes. As you do this, remember to have your conversations in a spirit of partnership and exploration. Avoid negative assessments that hold you or your teammates as "wrong." You are working together to develop your awareness, which is the first step in our revolution.

SECTION #2

The second part of the assignment is simple as well. For the next week, I want you to develop a new observing practice. The goal is to expand your awareness and set of distinctions about the world around you. Here is how it works. Each day of the week, put your attention on a new element of your world. For example, on day one you can focus on your yard. If you don't have a yard, then find a local park. Spend 5 minutes in your yard or the park and just notice what grabs your attention. Is it the trees, the grass, the shrubs, the flowers, the bugs, the people, or the wildlife? Then pick one or two objects or features, and focus your attention on them. What do you really notice about the color, shape, sounds, and smells? The goal is to notice something that you didn't notice at first glance. Drive beyond the mind's tendency to say, "A tree, big deal, I know what a tree is, let's get on to something interesting." Force yourself to disregard the internal chatter—especially the voice of your inner cynic—and keep your attention focused until you can distinguish something new. Maybe it is a nuance in the color, a gradation of shadow, a new layer of sound in the rustling of the leaves. I don't care what it is, but stay with the process until you are very clear that you have overcome your mind's tendency to dismiss what you are doing, and you have succeeded in observing something new.

The next day, do the same practice with a room in your house. After that, put your attention on your drive or ride to work. After that, your workplace. You get the point. For each day of the week, you have a new center of attention. Hold that attention until you are clear that you are observing something new, making new distinctions about your world. Again make some written notes about all of this, and if you have partners, compare notes with them. If not, save your notes as we will come back to them. I know I have been telling you that all along, and you might be wondering when. We will come back to them when we are at the end of the process, so please both make and keep your notes.

SECTION #3

Now things are going to get a bit more interesting. We are going to focus your attention on your internal landscape for a while. Again the practice is simple. But sticking with it will require that you confront your mind head-on, and that is never an easy task. Here you go. I am going to introduce you to a practice that we taught to Special Forces operators. It is called attention training. For the next 10 days, I want you to spend a mere 5 minutes a day as follows. Find a quiet place where you won't be disturbed. Sit in a chair with your arms and legs uncrossed, your back straight and not touching the back of the chair, and your chin level with the horizon. Gently close your eyes and start a simple breathing process, in through the nose and out through the mouth. That is all there is to the practice: in through the nose and out through the mouth. Once you have that going, which ought to be accomplished in two or three breaths, I then want you to put your attention on your breaths and track them with the simple thoughts of in and out. Not surprisingly, "in" is what you think on the in breath, and "out" is what you think on the out breath.

It sounds very simple, but what you will immediately notice is that your mind will begin to go crazy. It doesn't like discipline, so it will begin with all sorts of distracting thoughts and images; then the monologue will kick in. The internal critic will jump at the chance to say whatever it can to get you off purpose. Your job is just to keep coming back to "in" and "out." Nothing more, nothing less. Focus your attention on your breath and your process, and every time your mind distracts you, just notice it and let it go. Don't spend time criticizing yourself for having an inner critic, or worrying that you are somehow doing this "wrong." Just come back to your practice, again and again. You will be amazed at where your mind will go in the space of 5 short minutes—or how long 5 minutes can seem. Your goal is to keep your attention focused only on your process of in and out. Anything else is a distraction.

Ironically, another one of your mind's favorite tricks is to let you think you are doing well. *Hey, this is simple; I can do this, no problem!* That conversation is also a distraction. Let it go, along with your more critical thoughts, and come back to your process. When you are done, put your attention on two things. First, what do you notice about your body and your emotions? Second, what can you observe about the way your mind works to distract you? Make some notes about both of these and save them. At the end of a week you will be a different observer of yourself and have a bigger appreciation for what it takes to keep your attention focused.

SECTION #4

The next section of your assignment will be a bit more challenging, as you are now going to confront your inner cynic head-on. Here is the practice. For the next 10 days—yes, 10 days!—I want you to make a practice of carrying around something that you can write in or on. It could be a notepad, your Day-Timer, your PDA, whatever; it doesn't matter what you write on as long as you keep it with you. What you are going to do is use your awareness to begin to loosen the grip of your internal cynic. Your job is to wake up to the way it works. To do that, you must drive yourself to be aware. Each time you find yourself automatically reacting to some person, situation, or thing with a cynical response, make a note about it. What was it, what happened, what was your inner cynic telling you? You want to begin to notice patterns or categories of people or events that set it off. Now be alert here. Your mind will not want to do this and will come up with all sorts of reasons why this is dumb and pointless, why you don't really need to do it, certainly not for that long, etc. . . . Don't buy it! Drive yourself to make the notes, then take the next step. Pick one or two of the incidents *each day* and ask your mind what it was afraid of, such that it reacted in a cynical manner. The first response you will get will likely be something along the lines of, "I'm not being cynical, I am being realistic. You are just being foolish and wasting time." Don't be dissuaded, hang in there, and do the practice for 10 days. It will take that long for you to begin to get a grip on your cynic. By the time you are done, you should be able to see or feel the reaction coming and ask the question, "What are you afraid of?" quickly and in the moment. Once you get to that point, you will find that new possible ways of moving start to open up.

I want to be as clear as possible here. Your inner cynic isn't going to go quietly, so you will have to be vigilant and rigorous. The payoff is that you will have a new sense of freedom as you loosen its grip and a new ability to change both how you feel about the world around you and how you react or behave within it. This is a key step toward shaping the new you.

As always, make some notes about what you are observing as you go through the process. Save your notes and refer to them as you go along. They will give you a sense of the progress of your transformation and how the power to enact it is in your hands.

SEVEN

CHOICE: CLAIMING YOUR BIRTHRIGHT

> TRAVELER, THERE ARE NO PATHS.
> PATHS ARE MADE BY WALKING.
>
> —DON JUAN

I began this book by showing you the basic linguistic moves and the way that they shape our realities. In the last chapter we saw that being fully alive begins with becoming fully aware of ourselves and the people and the world around us. As our awareness grows, new worlds, both internal and external, open for us. Armed with awareness of the way our minds function, we discipline them to hone precise, powerful distinctions that afford us a wider range of responses to the challenges and opportunities that life dishes up. We discover that as our awareness expands, so does our range of choice. In every sense of the phrase, choice follows awareness.

Every day, every one of us makes a host of choices. This is another central element of being human. We have the awareness to make conscious choices. Every day, we make hundreds of small choices, choices we are often not fully aware that we are making. Over the course of our lives, we also have occasion to make choices that are clearly more conscious, substantial, and have an obvious, tremendous impact on where we go to school, where we live, how we earn a living, and how and with whom we spend our time. These major life choices demand all of our awareness and energy, as their consequences are clearly profound. In brief, as human beings, we spend every moment of every day making choices both large and small. My job is to wake you up to this reality and enable you to make more powerful choices.

The most fundamentally powerful declaration an individual can make is also the most basic: *I always have a choice*. This simple linguistic move shapes the context in which your entire life occurs, and it is the key to the process of enhancing personal power, performance, dignity, and grace: the building blocks of your transformation.

I always have a choice. If you look at your life from that declarative space, then you will see that everything that you are, everything that you do, everything that you have is the direct and sole result of the countless choices you have made during the course of your life. You choose your attitudes, opinions, beliefs, behavior, points of view, and responses to life. You choose your career path and your particular job. You choose all of your relationships and the condition of your relationships. Through your choices regarding eating, drinking, smoking, and exercise, you have chosen the state of your health, your bodily shape and appearance, and, to a significant degree, the length of your life. Ultimately, your entire life is a result of the choices you have made.

I realize that these are bold statements. That's the point. You aren't going to shape the new you by being timid. Already, just one page into this chapter, your mind has no doubt erupted with all sorts of reasons for why you don't always have a choice, exceptions to the statement, and ways that you are exempt from it. You are also likely awash in a flood of "what abouts" and "what ifs," which your mind wants to hide behind rather than own this powerful declaration. This reaction is only natural. I am inviting you to step into a new realm. If you live your life from the declaration *I always have a choice,* then you will find yourself living in a world that is very different from the one most of humanity inhabits.

Your mind naturally rebels at this notion. It would much rather avoid the discipline required to consistently be aware of all of the potential choices to be made, let alone be accountable for those choices you do make. If left to your conditioned responses, then you will quickly find yourself once again moving back into the herd and wondering why you ever bought this book in the first place. By now, I trust you know that comfort is not our goal. In fact, we are *consciously choosing* to move in the opposite direc-tion. I am pushing you to break free of your habitual patterns of seeing and being in the world.

I always have a choice: Let's take a deeper look at this funda-mental declaration and its profound implications.

The most challenging, and ultimately the most liberating, aspect of this declaration is its absoluteness. I am not offering you any back doors here. No exceptions, ifs, ands, or buts. To shape yourself and your world, this declaration has to be absolute. In each and every moment, you have a choice. What you do with those moments and those choices is up to you, but they are all yours. Every moment, you choose. There is no end to choosing and no escaping choice. You can see this as a blessing or a curse or accept it as it is intended: a challenge to rise to, a means to temper yourself and to forge a new you.

As you are reading this, your inner cynic is no doubt busy dishing up arguments and exceptions, hoping for a way out. Let me show you what I mean when I say there are no back doors by showing one example of how someone faced with an unpleasant circumstance might try to believe that he had no choice in the matter.

"I didn't choose to get fired from my job."

On the surface, this might seem to be the case. After all, what kind of an idiot would choose to get fired? Funny you should ask. It's likely that you didn't roll out of bed one morning, look in the mirror, and say, "That's it, I've had it. It's time to tell the boss to take this job and shove it. I choose to get fired, and today is the day. I don't care about the economy. I don't care about finding another job. I am done with that place!" Instead, over a period of weeks, months, or years, you made a series of incremental choices that produced the result of your getting fired. You chose, for example, to arrive late for work five times in the last 10 weeks. You chose to sit quietly in all the meetings where people were seeking ideas; you chose not to ask any questions about the strategy and direction of the company. Moreover, during the most recent quarter, you chose to miss your deadline on three important projects.

"Wait a minute!" your little voice howls in protest. "My tardiness wasn't my fault. I was only late for work so often because of all that terrible weather last winter, and because one morning the train broke down, and another morning my wife forgot to set the alarm clock. And those blown deadlines weren't all my fault. I finished my section of the draft on time. That the rest of the project team couldn't get their stuff done on time isn't my fault."

And so forth and so on. The voice in your head is defensive as well as cynical; it will fire up the excuse-o-matic in a heartbeat, and there will be no shortage of excuses. The problem is that's all they are: excuses. You choose to use them to hide behind rather than choosing to really manage all of the aspects of your work and career. In our world, that means you manage the nonfulfillment of your promises with as much rigor as you manage the fulfillment of them. Having an excuse or someone to blame, no matter how plausible, is *never* a substitute for fulfilling the commitments that you made to your manager and co-workers. By the same token, you chose to dismiss your boss as a jerk when she gave you a less-than-stellar performance review. You also chose to ignore the suggestions she made for your improvement, and you chose not to take any of the courses that the company made available for professional development. So, did you choose to get fired from your job? Absolutely. Were you awake and aware while you were making the choices that led to your dismissal? Absolutely not, and that too was your choice.

"I didn't choose to have my wife leave me."

Oh, really? Poor guy. She just up and left you like a bolt out of the blue. She never once let on that she was unhappy? She never said a word? Let's review this just a bit. Where and how have you spent your free time over the last several years? Did you choose to spend the bulk of it at home doing things with your wife and children, or did you chose to hide out on the golf course, at the tavern, at the ball game, or in front of the TV? Did you choose to talk about the ever-dimming flame of your sex life and how that felt, or did you choose to turn over angrily in bed and sulk? Let's keep going. You chose to grow that oh-so-attractive beer belly, ignore your wife's requests for an occasional intimate dinner out, and only on Valentine's Day did you choose to get her some flowers. There are thousands of books on how to enhance marriages, relationships, and your sex life, and you chose to read how many of them? Having fun yet? No, it's okay, there's more. You chose to forget your wedding anniversary, not to acknowledge her promotion, and you gave her a blender for her birthday! With these choices you have been undermining your marriage for years, and now you want to tell me that you didn't choose to have your wife leave you? It's way past time for you to wake up!

I can keep going, but I trust you are starting to see what I am pointing to. Every day we make hundreds of choices. Each and every one of these choices inescapably shapes both our present reality and our future. Most of them are small, and at least in the moment seem to have little consequence. The reality is that every choice we make, regardless of how small it may seem in the moment, opens and closes new futures. There is no way to tell what we may miss or experience in advance, and no way to predict how things will turn out. That doesn't change the reality that even the seemingly small choices we make shape our lives. Most people are blind to the impact that their choices have and thus don't pay much attention to the process of choosing on a day-to-day basis. This is something we are going to change.

Let's look at this claim—*I always have a choice*—from a different viewpoint. If I do not embody this declaration, then life occurs as a series of *"Have to's."* *"I have to* keep this crummy job." *"I have to* stay in this relationship." *"I have to* take my kids to school every day." *"I have to* take care of my parents." *"I have to* make all these payments every month." *"I have to* pay my taxes." *"I have to* go to school." Living life as an endless series of *"have to's"* produces a deep and profound mood of resentment and frustration. This, too, is a choice. The payoff for this choice is that you get to avoid accountability. The cost is that you feel out of control, powerless, overwhelmed, and victimized. Instead of being the master of your destiny, you are tossed on the waves of fate. This is not the way to shape a new you.

Sometimes you dither, procrastinate, analyze, consider, or otherwise put off making a choice. You choose not to choose. In the moment, it seems easy to justify, but one of two things will happen to you. The first is that if you choose not to choose, someone else will choose for you. You can then have someone to blame, but once again you chose to give up your power of choice; no one took it from you. You sat there and thought that life would wait while you made up your mind. It just doesn't work that way.

The other thing that happens is that you will be OBE—overcome by events. Life waits for none of us, and while you put off choosing, your field of choice narrows to the point where you don't like any of the choices. Your story becomes, "I don't have any choice." In fact, you had a host of choices in the beginning. You made one, which was that you chose to not choose, and now you don't like how that turned out. Well, as we all know (but sometimes choose to forget), there is no time-out in this game of life and only rarely do you get a do-over. These are clichés for a reason: because they hold truth.

It's time to go a bit deeper, as I suspect that you are still hanging on to some resistance to the notion that you always have a choice. Contrary to what you might think, I am not getting all Pollyanna on you. *I always have a choice* doesn't mean that you will always like all of the choices that you have. It doesn't work that way. You chose your way into being 30 pounds overweight, single, and alone, so having Brad Pitt invite you to Tahiti isn't on the menu. But you can still choose what you do next. Choose to put the pizza down, to start exercising, to deal with your savage inner critic that keeps telling you that you'll never be able to change so you might as well just give up. Choose to get your life back. Choose to get out in the world and have a social life. Put yourself in a position to make some bolder choices. Let me say it again: I am not trafficking in magic or fantasy.

One of the fundamental aspects of being an adult is seeing that as we make our choices, we open certain possibilities and close others. Maturity arrives when we realize that we may not be happy with all of our choices and their outcomes, but we can be at peace with them.

Using your awareness to consciously make choices is not always easy or fun. But it is powerful, and that is the point. *"I always have a choice"* isn't THE TRUTH; it is a declaration that I make. It is a stand that I take that enables me to move in the world in ways that others cannot.

Let's consider another example of someone in a position she doesn't want to be in, a slightly more complex situation than the two I outlined earlier. A division manager of a large corporation has just been informed that her major project has been cancelled, which means that her operating budget will be cut, and she will have to lay off employees. Did she choose to have her project cancelled? Not consciously, but rather than walk through the decision tree again, let's go with, "No, she didn't." "But wait," you might be arguing, "you said I always have a choice, and now you're admitting that she didn't choose that!" I didn't say you get to choose everything. I said you always have a choice. That means that right now, in this moment, you have a choice. What choices does our manager have right now? She may choose to dispute the decision with her superiors, worry about her own position, and take this as more evidence for why you can't trust senior management. That choice will take her deeper into cynicism, steer her off center, and diminish her future career possibilities. On the other hand, she can choose to use the setback as an opportunity to honestly reassess her own performance, the status of her career, and the best moves to make for herself and her family. She can choose to introduce her employees to new career opportunities, generate an offer for a new project, and manage her inner cynic so that she stays ambitious and optimistic, and avoids the siren call of cynicism.

Often when I'm working on this principle during a session with a corporate group, one of the participants will propose a much darker hypothetical as a "what about." Let's go on that ride for a moment.

"What about if you're in a plane that's been hijacked? You certainly didn't choose that set of circumstances. And now that the plane is only a few minutes away from crashing, you're not left with any choice at all."

I consider this for a moment and try to show the participants how this example still fits within my claim that we always have choices we can make.

"I can see why it might look that way," I reply. "It is not likely that you woke up this morning and said, '*Ah, this is a good day to die, and I choose to make it dramatic by having my flight hijacked and crashed.*' So let's stay with your scenario. You didn't choose to have your plane hijacked, but it has been hijacked nonetheless. You are about to die, and there is no way to avoid that. In the moment, it may seem that you have no choice, but let's look a bit closer and remember, I didn't say you get to choose everything, and I didn't say you will always have choices that you like. What I said, and what I still hold to be true, is this: *I always have a choice.* Even in these dire circumstances, holding on to that declaration keeps you in a position of power. What choices do you have, even in what may appear to be your final moments? Well, like the passengers on United 93, you can choose to resist and fight. You may not get control of the plane, but you can choose to die fighting and not as a helpless victim. You may choose to call your family on your cell phone and leave a farewell message. You may choose to use these moments to pray and make your peace with your god. You may choose to use the opportunity to center yourself and see what fate dishes up. Even as the plane is careering toward the ground, you still have choices. Do you die cursing the hijackers, or do you find it in your heart to forgive them?"

As grim as the alternatives may be, as a human being, you have the ultimate declarative authority in your life. You get to choose. Tyrants, bureaucrats, and clerics of all sorts have attempted throughout history to disavow you of this notion. You may choose to give up your power of choice, but no one can take it away from you. No matter how dark things may seem in any given moment, you still have a choice.

On a lighter note, let's consider the choices available to the man reluctantly attending his first modern dance performance with his wife. Our reluctant guy has decided before the performance that he doesn't like this sort of thing, and he resents being dragged away from the big football game on TV. Every office in the country is full of guys who are Monday-morning victims. Every Monday morning, at the first opportunity, they will lament the "fact" that they didn't have any choice but to go to—you can fill in the blank—because their wives insisted on it. In their story, they had no choice, but by now we all know that they did. They chose to attend whatever it was and deal with the probability that it would be unpleasant rather than deal with their upset wives and the certainty that would be unpleasant. Remember, I didn't say that you always have choices you will like. So while our reluctant dance attendee may live in a story in which he didn't choose to go to the performance, we all know that he did.

Once at the performance, he has a new range of choices. He can choose to keep his resentful mood and suffer through the performance, finding not even the slightest thing to enjoy about it. He can choose to wake up and make a game out of finding something that he likes about it. He can choose to learn something about modern dance and read the program, study the moves of the performers, and pay attention to the interplay of movement, light, music, and costume. If he has been doing the exercises in this book, he can choose to hone his awareness and think about how the enemies of learning and his own lazy mind might be preventing him from enjoying something new. If these attempts at understanding fail, he can choose just to close his eyes and listen to the music. The entire performance is rife with opportunities to choose. I know this doesn't bode well for the Monday-morning victims, but when did whining become a national pastime?

Whether the choice is minor or critical, whether the range of options is wide or narrow, *I always have a choice,* and here are some key elements that are critical to bear in mind:

- Choice follows awareness. To increase my field of choices, I must first declare that I always have a choice, and then expand my awareness to see new possibilities. I can't choose what I can't see.

- When I declare that I choose everything in my life, I take full ownership of my personal power.

- When I hear my inner cynic saying, "I don't have any choice about this," it is an indication that I'm not using all of my awareness. In fact, I am probably casting about for an easy way out.

- I can approach any situation and look for choices. The powerful position is to look for the "highest option." What is the best outcome that can occur in these circumstances? I then choose that option and move to make it so.

Let's now focus our attention on what typically inhibits our willingness to make conscious choices. Each time we make a choice, it produces a result. We typically refer to these results as the consequences of our choices. Consequences are neither good nor bad; they are simply the results of our choices. Making a choice that results in your intended consequence or a desirable consequence doesn't mean you are a good person, nor does making a choice that results in an unintended or undesirable consequence make you a bad person.

The tendency to assess everything as either good or bad is overly simplistic and can be quite destructive. Here is why I say that. Most people have trouble distinguishing themselves from their choices. They cannot make the distinction between "I made a bad choice," and "I am a bad person." While it may be natural or easy to collapse these two things together, this reductive thinking lacks rigor and produces only paralysis as we succumb to the inner voice telling us how wrong and bad we are for being so dumb, naive, lazy, etc. A steady stream of this acidic discourse eats away at your dignity and causes you to choose more timidly. We choose to diminish ourselves rather than take the risk of being made wrong first by ourselves and then by others. This process is insidiously incremental. You don't notice it as you slowly shut yourself down. You aren't awake to the choices that you make to constrict instead of expand as you go through life. Then, if you are lucky, one morning in middle age you wake up to discover that, day by day, your choices have produced a life that has very little resemblance to your dreams, desires, and ambitions. Remember when I brought up the choice-point moment so many of us have faced when we suddenly wonder: *Whose life is this? How did I get here?* You got here as a result of the choices you made, aware or unaware.

Let's say, for example, that I'm out for a hike on a beautiful summer afternoon. I'm wearing hiking boots, and my feet are getting a bit hot and sweaty. Off the trail, beyond a broad meadow of luxuriant knee-high grass and bright wildflowers, I see a swiftly rushing mountain stream. Choosing to leave the trail, I hurry across the meadow to get a bit of relief by soaking my feet in the stream. Halfway across the meadow, I savor the aroma of the grass and flowers and eagerly anticipate the feel of the water coursing over my bare feet. While engrossed in my thoughts, I am not paying attention to where I am walking, and I step squarely into a large, freshly deposited meadow muffin (i.e., a steaming pile of cow flop). What am I going to do? I could stand in the middle of the cow crap and berate myself. "Oh man, I can't believe you did that, what a moron. Why don't you watch where you are going? You jerk, how are you going to get this off your boots, what a loser, you made a bad choice." While I am wasting all of this time listening to this diatribe by my inner critic, I'm also sinking deeper into the dung. A better choice would be to notice that I inadvertently took a step into something unpleasant, shake it off (literally and figuratively), and take another step that will bring me closer to my goal of getting to the stream.

In this example, it is very easy to see how beating myself up, wallowing in self-criticism, and making myself wrong contributes absolutely nothing toward achieving my goal and, in fact, serves no purpose at all. But we do this to ourselves on a daily basis, often without even noticing it. We make choices that do not produce the intended result, and rather than simply making another choice, we attack ourselves or listen to others do it for us, and in so doing take ourselves out of the game.

Remember one of our axioms from centering: Energy follows attention. When you put all of your attention on attacking yourself, that is where your energy goes, and this will only exacerbate the bad situation and make you feel worse. Calling your emotional travel agent to book a guilt trip is just a waste of time. The challenge for all of us is to accept that as human beings, a great many of our choices will produce results that we didn't intend. This doesn't mean that the choice was bad, or that I am bad for making it. It merely means that I need to make a different choice if I want to produce my intended results. Of course you want to learn from each choice that you make, but you don't learn anything from judging yourself as "bad."

To assess yourself or others as "bad" carries a nasty, negative, moralistic overtone that serves no purpose. The self-righteous and power-hungry use this assessment to frighten and intimidate others. "Don't be bad" is simply a code they use for, "Do what I tell you to do." In the end, there are no bad choices; your choice produces either a desired or undesired result. My choice to leave the trail and walk across the meadow, for instance, produced a desired result: I enjoyed the aroma of the wildflowers, and the shortcut delivered me to the stream where I luxuriously soaked my sweaty feet. By contrast, my choice to take the shortest route across the meadow, through the tallest grass, produced an undesired result: I stepped in the cow flop. Seeing no point to standing there, sinking deeper into it, I laughed and chose to keep on walking.

It is easy to see how athletes suffer when they succumb to self-blame. I use sports metaphors and examples not because they are so profound but because they are easy to understand, and this approach to shaping the new you began from our work with athletes. In that work, I could readily spot a player who had taken himself out of the game by attacking himself for making a choice that had resulted in an unintended result. After he missed a shot or made an errant throw, his inner critic had a field day, and while the two of them took a time-out to discuss his failings as a player, the other team kept playing the real game. Golfers are notorious in this regard. The long delay between shots provides too much time for useless self-recrimination.

Here is an example from my own personal experience. When I was younger, I was a serious rugby player. I started my career as an undergraduate at the University of Washington, in Seattle, and after graduating I played with Old Puget Sound Beach, a Seattle-based club that fields a number of teams. If you're unfamiliar with rugby, it's a fast-paced game of continuous motion, more like basketball or soccer than American football. When a rugby player makes an ill-fated play, he doesn't have the luxury of sitting around and beating himself up. If he does, then the other team will pounce, making things worse. One member of our team was an immensely talented athlete, fast and explosive, but unfortunately unwilling to manage his emotions. During one key moment in a big game, he made a bad pass, lost the ball, and chose to indulge in a self-abusive wig-out, dropping to his knees and slapping his forehead, ripping himself for his "bad" play. During his pointless theatrics, the opposing team took advantage of his distraction to score.

This same thing happens all too often in your life. While you are busy attacking yourself for something you think you did "wrong," the game of life keeps moving. The game doesn't stop for anyone, and in today's complex and competitive world, you simply can't afford to take yourself out of play. There are enough formidable forces and opponents for us to contend with as it is. We don't need to wear the other team's colors.

On one end of the scale, we have our hotheaded rugger who doesn't consider the consequences that his choice to indulge his emotions might have on his team. On the other end, we find the growing legion of people who are reluctant to make any choice at all. This timidity has reached near epidemic proportions in corporate America, where the confident captains of industry of an earlier era have been replaced by risk-adverse analysts and caretaking bureaucrats. Rather than boldly commit to any strong choice, these politically correct managers form committees as, they say, "We want to be sure everyone has a voice in the decision." The committees, in turn, hold a series of meetings and eventually establish a bland consensus that frees any individual from accountability. The committee then issues a set of recommendations. By the time these recommendations reach the desk of the CEO, however, the world has shifted: The business opportunity has passed, the range of choices has narrowed, and the recommendations are largely useless, so the process starts again.

We dither and agonize over making the "right" choice, when there is no such thing. There are only more- and less-powerful and effective choices. There are no "right" ones. Each choice you make, no matter how small, shifts the entire field of possibilities and opens up new choices. Rather than endlessly agonizing over making the *right* choice, you are often better off making the *best* choice, the one that, however imperfect, in the moment moves you closer to your goal. After assessing the consequences of your current choice, you are then better positioned to make the next one.

Move. Make a choice. If it doesn't produce the result you intended, then recalibrate and choose again. There is no other path to creating the new you.

ASSIGNMENT #5

FOUR SECTIONS
TIME TO COMPLETE: 15 DAYS

Choices: We all make them constantly and often unconsciously. To some extent this is understandable, as you don't want to spend energy and attention on choosing to breathe, blinking your eyes, or taking each step. If we consciously made every choice in our lives, then we'd be paralyzed by the immense number of choices that we have to make. Thankfully our bodies have a wisdom of their own and have relieved us of much of that burden. At the same time, we all too often go on autopilot when making choices that have a much bigger impact on us. Thus the first part of your assignment is intended to help you be more aware when you make choices.

SECTION #1

For the next 3 or 4 days, keep a little log of at least five clear, conscious choices that you make each day. In this case, "clear" and "conscious" mean that you spent some time looking at alternatives and intentionally made a choice. I am not interested in the magnitude of the choice. It could be decaf instead of regular, large curd over small, or Ford not Chevy. What matters is that you made a clear choice. For each of these choices, make some written notes that detail at least three possibilities that your choice opened and three possibilities that it closed. Remember that open is not better than closed. I simply want to begin to train you to observe some of the implications of your choices. This is a means to expanding your awareness. If you are working with a partner or team, set aside some time to share what you wrote and what you are beginning to see about the phenomenon of choosing.

SECTION #2

Let's do some work in the other direction. With the same log that you used above, I want you to do the following. At the end of each day, make a list of at least 10 choices that you made during the day that you can see, upon reflection, were largely unconscious. Don't include bodily functions. Instead, look at your day and note, for example, that you made an unconscious choice about the route that you took to get to work. It is the same way that you go every day, and you just got into the car and drove. You won't have to spend much time to find 10 of these choices. Once you have your list, pick four of them and do the same thing that you did with the first list. Make a note of possibilities that each choice opened and possibilities that it closed.

SECTION #3

Now let's turn our attention to the areas of life where you may live in a story in which you don't have any choice, where you "have to." It may be that by now you have come to see that there is no aspect of life in which you have no choice. As noted, you may not always like the choices that are in front of you, but you do always have a choice. If you can really own that declaration, then we are clearly making progress. But most of us hold on to the notion that there are aspects of our lives in which we have little choice. If that group includes you, then let's do the following. Make a list of 5 to 10 things that you truly believe you "have to do." After each item on your list, write what you think would happen if you didn't do it. Think of it this way. If you put "I have to pay my taxes" on your list, then think of it in terms of "then what?" If you don't pay your taxes, then what is going to happen? Perhaps the IRS will take your money and put you in jail. Good answer—that is exactly what I am looking for. Then what? "Then I won't be able to take care of my family." Good, keep going. Make your list, and then for each item do at least four to five levels of "then whats." Once you have completed the list of "have tos" and "then whats," pause for a moment and read it all. As you are doing this, I want you to focus your awareness on how you are feeling. What emotions does the list evoke? Don't gloss over this, as it is a critical element of what we are up to. Be very clear with yourself about the emotional state you're left in after writing and reading through this list. Most people will find that they are resentful, angry, cynical, depressed, or resigned as a result of all of the things they "have to" do. Any and all of these are both normal and expected reactions. Don't be embarrassed by these feelings or think that they ought to be different.

The next step is to take that same list, and for each of your "have tos," do the following: Write them as clear declarative choices. Write, "I choose to pay my taxes. I choose to avoid an IRS tax lien. I choose to stay out of jail." When you have your list complete, there is one final step. You have now made clear volitional choices. I want you to notice that in each case you can see that what you have held as a "have to" has all along been a choice. The truth is that I choose to pay my taxes rather than go to jail. The term rather makes it clear that you have a choice. You always did. When you have completed your list and this contextual scan of it, again bring your awareness to your emotions. What feelings does this list generate as distinct from the first list? Make some written notes on this experience and the emotions that it generated, and share the notes with your partners.

SECTION #4

The final element in this assignment is designed to bring more awareness to your choices. For the next 10 days you are to do the following practice: Each day make 100 declarations of choice. It doesn't matter how big or small the choices are, the goal is to solidly anchor the declaration: *I always have a choice.* The practice is simple. All you have to do is say to yourself, "I choose to _____."

"I choose to wear black today." "I choose to have Grape-Nuts and berries for breakfast." "I choose to go to this meeting." "I choose to make this call." What you are choosing doesn't matter; the fact that you are choosing does. Make these declarations of choice to yourself, and after you have done this for 10 days, 100 times a day, make some written notes on what you are beginning to notice about your mood and outlook on life. Be alert to your inner cynic as he or she will work to tell you why this is silly and/or why you don't need to do it. Choose to thank the cynic for being concerned, and let him or her know that you are choosing to ignore this critical little voice.

————————————————

EIGHT

ABILITY AND WILLINGNESS

IF I WERE TO WISH FOR ANYTHING, I SHOULD NOT
WISH FOR WEALTH AND POWER, BUT FOR THE
PASSIONATE SENSE OF THE POTENTIAL, FOR THE EYE
WHICH, EVER YOUNG AND ARDENT, SEES THE POSSIBLE.
PLEASURE DISAPPOINTS, POSSIBILITY NEVER!
—KIERKEGAARD

In the last chapter, I showed you how the declaration *I always have a choice* gives you the power to act consciously, with clarity and conviction, which is a key part of shaping the new you. Now we are going to talk about a second crucial declaration: *I am inherently able.*

What does this mean? This means that given the limitations of your human body, which every day, we find, are far fewer and far less substantial than we thought, you are able to do anything that you choose. You live in a world where the only limits are the ones that you place on yourself. What you may once have considered to be impenetrable barriers to accomplishment in any realm exist only in your mind.

I know these are bold statements and that once again we are going to contend with an internal chorus of "No I can't, he's crazy, what a bunch of bull." It's okay—I am used to the nay-saying inner critic, and by now you should be too. At the same time, I hope you are also getting used to proving him or her wrong. You do have the power to change, to shape a new you, and, chapter by chapter, you're getting the tools you need to do just that. *I am inherently able* is a strong declaration and stands side by side with *I always have a choice*. Once you realize the power of these two declarations, you'll be able to make them manifest in your life and tear through whatever limitations you may have been imposing upon yourself—knowingly or not—up until now.

Let's talk a little bit about the limitations you've been placing upon yourself. Every day we are bombarded with a host of messages that subtly seek to undermine your belief in your own ability. The media point relentlessly to your inadequacy. You can't protect yourself: You need the government to do that. You can't manage your finances: You need Wall Street. You can't lose weight: You need this or that pill, diet, video, and health club. You can't live your own values and build your own spiritual connection: You need organized religion. You can't find love: You need the Internet. The list goes on and on and on, numbing us to its incrementally debilitating effect. The fact is that these fixes are all for sale, and in order to be sold something, we first have to believe that we have a deficit, a lack that needs filling. Advertisers invest tens of billions of dollars every year to convince you that you aren't able to make it on your own.

We began as a nation of pioneers, rebels, and adventurers. We built this country out of the collective belief that there was nothing that we could not do, there were no limits, and we did it on our own. In fact, if you look at the history of the United States, you'll see that it is largely a roll call of those who sought to accomplish what was at the time said to be impossible.

Hollywood would have us believe that our historical heroes are somehow larger than life and made of different stuff than the rest of us, and that they live in some rarified world that is closed to all but the mighty few. On the contrary, these pioneering spirits and heroes are not larger than life, nor are they a thing of the past. Their spirit is still within us, and that capacity for greatness is still among us.

Are we all not made of the same stuff as the founding fathers, the great explorers, the great spiritual and political leaders of the country? Of course we are. You and Lance Armstrong, Wilma Rudolph, Thomas Jefferson, Abraham Lincoln, Albert Einstein, and Rosa Parks are all cut from the same cloth. Are we "ordinary people" of today any less capable of greatness than these heroes? Of course not. There is so much evidence to support the declaration that as human beings we are inherently able that to believe otherwise is simply irrational.

So what does set history's revered characters and today's great leaders apart from the rest of us? Put simply, the great leaders, soldiers, scientists, artists, athletes, and performers of any age fundamentally believe that they can achieve whatever they set their minds to. Armed with this belief, they build a set of practices for accomplishing their goals, and the result is, as they say, history. If you are willing to make this same declaration—that you are capable of whatever you set your mind to—and if you then bring it to life with your actions, then you too can accomplish whatever it is that you hold to be greatness.

What does it mean to say that *I am inherently able*?

Let's start by understanding what it doesn't mean. It doesn't mean that in the current moment, I am completely competent to accomplish anything I choose. Remember—I'm not dispensing magic pills. What it does mean is that you are infinitely capable of learning and becoming competent. If you are willing to invest the time and do the work, then you are able to learn to do anything.

This notion that *I am inherently able* might make sense on an abstract intellectual level, but chances are your little inner critic is still sounding off. "You must be kidding, I am not in the same league as these people you are pointing to! I would like to believe it, but it just isn't so." Notice the key word in the sentence: believe. That is what we're talking about here, a belief, a declaration that reshapes everything that you are and do. A belief might sound vague and intangible, but this one—the belief that you are inherently able—opens the door to a new world and provides you with choices you might never have dreamed of.

Consider the example of an organization called Students Run L.A., which operates in affiliation with the Los Angeles Unified School District. Each school year, SRLA takes hundreds of sedentary, nonathletic teenagers from Southern California's most disadvantaged areas and over a 6-month period trains them to complete a marathon. When the students attend the introductory SRLA meeting in September and learn that a marathon is 26.2 miles long, most simply laugh and walk away. Even the ones who remain don't believe they will be able to achieve this seemingly impossible goal; most of them can't even run around the block. They simply do not hold themselves as able. They have fallen prey to society's covert message that they are deficient, and they exist in an environment in which they rarely receive positive reinforcement. As we all know, kids are ruthless with each other, and when you combine that tendency for put-down humor and teasing with a lack of solid role models, no affirmative support, and a media onslaught that works to disempower us all, it is little wonder that these kids hold themselves as unable.

With the help of committed coaches, however, the kids who do stick with the program learn to make distinctions, expand their awareness, believe in themselves, and make powerful choices toward accomplishing their goal of running a marathon. None of this would be possible if they did not hold themselves as able. To be sure, in the early stages of the program, it is largely the coaches who hold the belief in the students' ability and not the kids. To them, running 26.2 miles seems impossible. But you know what? Walking around the block isn't. Once a kid has done that for a few days, he or she can make it two blocks, then six, and after that, he or she can run one and walk two, and then run one and walk one, and then run two and walk one. In no time the kids are running a mile, then a 10-K. Along the way, they learn to make better choices regarding nutrition, sleep, and schoolwork. Day by day, choice by choice, the students become more competent runners. When the marathon day finally comes around in March, more than 90 percent of the kids who have gone through the SRLA program are able to run and complete the entire 26.2 miles. These profoundly ordinary, previously incompetent, unfit young people have achieved something extraordinary. What should we take away from their story?

- Personal empowerment begins when I hold myself as able.

- Team empowerment begins when I hold others as able.

The essential issue here is personal power. Put simply, it is much more powerful to hold myself as able than unable. When I hold myself as able, everything is on the menu and I can choose. If I am not able, or if I limit the realms in which I hold myself as able, then I have neither choice nor power. If I am able, then whether or not I attain a certain goal is merely a matter of my willingness. And willingness is a matter of choice.

Let's keep exploring. My claim is that willingness is a matter of choice. Therefore the declaration "I choose not to" is infinitely more powerful than "I can't." "I can't" suggests some outside limitation or obstacle, and the weight of history says that these obstacles exist only in my mind. Again, the world of sports offers many dramatic examples of this principle. Perhaps the most famous one,

one that has inspired people in all endeavors, was the breaking of the 4-minute-mile barrier by the British runner Roger Bannister in 1954. For as long as athletes had been running the mile, the 4-minute barrier was considered impregnable. Coaches told their runners that it was impossible for a human being to cover the distance in less than that time. Medical experts agreed, warning that any athlete who attempted to break the barrier would pay with his life. Over time, the 4-minute mile grew into an imposing psychological barrier and became a symbol of the presumed scientific limits on all human performance.

Through the 1930s, '40s, and early '50s, runners inched ever closer to the 4-minute mark, yet the barrier remained in place. Never mind that increasing numbers of athletes logged times just a second or two slower than 4 minutes with no ill effects; the 4-minute mark was deemed absolutely inviolate. Then along came Bannister, an English medical student, who methodically trained to break the record. Finally, on May 6, 1954, he achieved the historic goal.

In achieving his presumably impossible goal, Bannister opened the floodgates. Within months after his achievement, a half-dozen other runners also surpassed the formerly impregnable standard. Roger Bannister broke the record, but more importantly, he broke apart the belief system that was responsible for holding it in place as a limitation of human potential for so long.

Another dramatic example is the rise of women's sports over the last 30 years. As recently as 1980, for instance, there were no running events longer than 1500 meters for women at the Olympic Games. The common wisdom held that women somehow weren't capable of running as far as men. We now know that to be nonsense, and since 1984 women have been happily running the same Olympic events as men and rapidly closing the performance gaps.

Who knows which of our widely accepted "facts" about human limitations will seem just as nonsensical 25 years from now? To put it in terms of our basic linguistic moves, this is what happens when we treat an assessment as an assertion. We confuse what is essentially a long-held opinion with a fact.

At HP2 we have done a lot of work with all sorts of high-performing teams over the years. In part, what enables them to be high-performing teams is that each member declares him- or herself as able and holds the rest of the team as able, too. This doesn't mean that each member of the team is equally competent, but rather that respect for each individual's ability forms the starting point for mutual support and effective coaching. When I hold others as able, I empower both the individual and the team within which the individual operates.

When a manager takes the stand that her team is able, she is willing to give them additional responsibilities and let go of control. She functions creatively as a coach, rather than restrictively as a boss. When the members of a team know that their leader trusts and believes in them, they can achieve spectacular results.

On the other end of that scale, we have the manager who doesn't hold his team as able and who typically receives less than stellar work from them, a direct result of this lack of belief in their abilities. This is typically the guy who insists on constantly checking everyone's work, micromanaging every project, and who, when the slightest hint of missing a deadline appears, takes over and does things himself. He then complains about being overwhelmed and doesn't understand why his people won't put in any extra effort or don't seem to perform to the level of their peers.

This unfortunate example of how a lack of belief in others' ability limits their capacity to perform is not restricted to business or sports. Consider the story of two elementary-school teachers who were both assigned classes of students that had amassed nearly identical mid-range academic records. However, for the purposes of the experiment, one teacher was told that the children in her class were academically gifted, while the other teacher was told that his students were all working below grade level. By the end of the school year, the "gifted" students had all made significant gains and were performing well above grade level. The "slow" students in the second class, by contrast, had all lost ground and were in fact performing below grade level. Each class, in short, had lived up or down to the expectations of its teacher. One class was held as able, and the other as unable, and they performed to those expectations.

On a grander scale, consider President Kennedy's famous declaration of 1961 that within a decade, America would put a man on the moon. Until President Kennedy made that declaration, space travel of any sort was restricted to the realm of science fiction. At that point in time we had less than 10 percent of the technology it would take to get the job done. Were we competent to put a man on the moon? No. But because Kennedy both declared the mission and held the engineers and scientists as able to see it through, he provided the context in which they would develop both the competence and the technology to accomplish the mission. Before the 1960s were over, Neil Armstrong had walked on the moon and the nation had justified its late president's faith in its collective ability.

By holding both myself and other people as able, I empower myself and others to perform at an extraordinary level.

If you are inherently able, then there is nothing that you "can't" do. Let's spend just a little more time discussing the fundamental distinction between "I can't" and "I choose not to," and how this relates to the idea that you are inherently able. "I can't" is ultimately a victim statement. It suggests that there is some insurmountable barrier out there in the world that is somehow constraining you, some malevolent power that is holding you back. But when I hold myself as inherently able, then the choice to be unwilling to do something is just that: my choice. When I consciously choose to say no, I am enhancing my personal power. To test this, simply take stock of how you feel when you make each of the two statements. "I can't" tends to produce a feeling, however slight, of helplessness. "I choose not to" leaves you feeling in control.

To be sure, "I can't" has become a common conversational move, but oftentimes it is just something we hide behind. When you say, "I can't make it for lunch on Tuesday," you don't literally mean that it would be impossible for you to make it. You could, but for whatever reason—valid or not—you are unwilling to rearrange your schedule to be there. "I can't get this report done by next week." Yes you can, but are you willing to do what it would take to get it done? "I can't learn to ski at this point in life." Yes you can, but are you willing to put in the time and go through the process of being a beginner in order to learn? "I can't go out and find a new job." Yes you can, but are you willing to take the risk and go through the process? What you want to notice here is the tendency not to own your choices. We want to hide behind "I can't" rather than be straight about what we are or are not willing to do.

Every time I say "I can't," I disempower and diminish myself, and I provide myself with an excuse for not taking a risk. Declaring yourself as unable, "I can't," takes you off the hook and out of the game. You don't have to extend yourself. You don't have to deal with being a beginner in some new realm and risk looking awkward, foolish, and incompetent. At the same time, by declaring yourself unable, you narrow your range of choices, limit your awareness, abdicate your personal power, and rob yourself of the opportunity to learn.

The list of possibilities which are legitimately beyond our abilities is, in fact, very short. Now, just to be clear, I am not suggesting that you should climb every mountain simply because you can. What I am pointing to is this: If you hold yourself as able to climb any mountain, then you will be able to move through any mountain range with confidence rather than anxiety. "I know that I can climb any of these mountains, so there is nothing to be anxious about. I choose not to climb them now."

The declaration "I can't," in short, is not on the menu for the new you. It has no role in your transformation. "I choose not to," by contrast, is a perfectly legitimate declaration. It is, in fact, one that I recommend you make often. No more hiding behind "I can't." Short of the fantasy realm, there is no such thing. At the age of 58, I am not going to play in the NBA. Like all humans, I am bound by the limitations of my particular body and age. However, that doesn't mean I can't play basketball. If I am willing to do the work, I can still become the best player possible within my limitations. I can choose to practice shooting and dribbling, to lift weights, and to work on my flexibility and agility. I can run to increase my endurance and join an adult basketball league. Or, with equal power and dignity, I can choose not to pursue basketball. I am able but unwilling. It is my choice. There is no "I can't."

It is especially critical to understand this distinction and its longterm implications when working with children. For example, I have a 12-year-old daughter named Cheyenne. Like many kids, she is often reluctant to attempt new things. Her opening response to many new activities or opportunities is "I can't," a declaration that sets her on a course that is not rich in possibilities. And, like most dads, I have learned tactics to help my daughter see herself as able. If, like the students in the marathon-training program in Los Angeles, Cheyenne starts moving in small increments toward a new goal rather than viewing it as a single monumental task, when she takes even a tentative first step into a new activity, her adamant "I can't" gradually softens into a grudging, "Okay, I'll try it," and eventually transforms into an affirmative, "Yes, I can." Armed with some successes, she then becomes more willing to attempt new things as she begins to hold herself as able.

Often "I can't" is a cover for "I am afraid to." Rather than own our fear, which is itself a powerful move—as we can't work with our fear until we acknowledge it—we hide behind the lie of inability. Over time we forget that "I can't" is nothing but a story we have made up for our own comfort and convenience. The danger here is that we forget we made it up and start to believe that it's the truth. This is where we need to hone our awareness and wake up!

Are you able to have the relationship you always wanted? Yes, you are. Are you able to have the career you set your sights on? Yes, you are. Are you able to have a healthy, fit body? Yes, you are. Are you able to do anything you set your sights on? Yes, you are. Are you able to shape a new you? Are you able to transform yourself and have a new future? Yes, you are! Are you willing?

ASSIGNMENT #6

FIVE SECTIONS
TIME TO COMPLETE: 10 DAYS

If you have been keeping up with the assignments, then you will have begun to notice that you are looking at your world a bit differently. That is a very good sign, as it means that the process is working and your transformation is under way. We of course want to sustain that good work, so let's keep moving.

SECTION #1

Let's begin with a quick check on the enemies of learning. As you may have figured out by now, we are going to keep revisiting this conversation. They won't rest, and you can't let down your guard. You can't have made it this far without engaging in some serious battles with your enemies of learning. Make some notes on which of them seem to be consistent visitors and what it is that you are doing to keep them at bay. Are you constantly finding yourself confused and impatient? Do you keep falling into ongoing assessments? Are you still fending off "I can't do this, it's too hard, too complex, takes too long"? What is important to note is that you have your sights set on something that is more important and compelling than the siren call of your enemies of learning.

Make some notes and be sure you share them with your partners. This is the power of working together as a learning team. You can support each other when you are grabbed by the enemies of learning.

SECTION #2

To return to some other ideas we discussed in earlier chapters, please make a quick written report on the status of your centering practice. Are you doing your daily two-steps? Your assignment was

to do them every day. Yes, every day. If so, then what are you noticing about your practice? How do those two-steps feel now? What
is the internal conversation that you find yourself in while you are
doing them? While you are getting ready to do them? What standards do you use to assess that you are getting better at the two-
step, and finally, how do you see that this practice is affecting your
life? If you are not doing the practice, then what is the story that
your inner cynic sold you to let yourself off the hook? "I didn't
understand I was supposed to do them every day." "I'm too busy."
"I've already got it down." Since any story that results in your not
doing the practice is unacceptable, what are you going to do to get
back on track, and when today are you going to do your practice?

SECTION #3

For the next week you are going to focus your attention on your
tendency to fall into "I can't." The method for doing so is simple
and by now, I hope, predictable. Keep a daily log of the conversations in which you use the phrase. I don't expect a transcript of
every conversation you have, but I do want you to make notes
about the circumstances in which those words come out of your
mouth. If you sharpen your awareness, then you will be surprised
at how often this happens. For each "I can't," write down what you
see that it was a cover for. The choices are essentially "I am afraid
to," "I am currently not competent to/at," or "I am unwilling to."
The object here is to bring your awareness to the conditioned tendency of using "I can't" as a hiding place.

SECTION #4

The last thing to write about is how you feel when you say, "I
can't." This requires a keen awareness, so pay careful attention to
your body and your emotions. The distinctions we are working on
now are subtle but very powerful. See if you can notice how each
time you say "I can't," you feel slightly diminished, just a tiny bit

resigned, or just incrementally worse about yourself. This is important, so don't gloss over it. It may well be that you are numb to the effects, and that is all right. If you really don't notice any effect or emotion, write that down too.

SECTION #5

Finally, we are going to shift directions and work on embodying these new distinctions. After you have completed your single week of logging "I can'ts," turn your attention to saying instead, "I choose not to." Make a point of catching yourself prior to saying "I can't," and shift it to "I choose not to," or "I am unwilling to do that," or "I am currently not competent at . . ." The goal is to reclaim yourself from the lie of inability and own your inherent capacity to learn and accomplish. Make a log of at least 10 occasions over the course of 2 or 3 days in which you consciously change "I can't" into one of these more powerful statements. With each of these entries, make an additional note about how you felt when you made the more powerful statement. Again, it is critical that you anchor in your mind/body the emotional payoff for holding yourself as able and making clear choices.

As always, if you are working with a partner or team, share your notes and have a conversation in which you talk about what you are learning and what you see is shifting in your life. If you don't have a partner, then take notes and save them as we will come back to them at the end of our process.

NINE

ACCOUNTABILITY

> THE CREDIT BELONGS TO THE MAN WHO IS
> ACTUALLY IN THE ARENA . . . WHO STRIVES
> VALIANTLY, WHO KNOWS THE GREAT ENTHUSIASMS,
> THE GREAT DEVOTIONS, AND SPENDS HIMSELF IN
> WORTHY CAUSES. WHO, AT BEST, KNOWS THE
> TRIUMPH OF HIGH ACHIEVEMENT AND WHO, AT
> WORST, IF HE FAILS, FAILS WHILE DARING GREATLY
> SO THAT HIS PLACE SHALL NEVER BE WITH THOSE
> COLD AND TIMID SOULS WHO KNOW NEITHER
> VICTORY NOR DEFEAT.
> —TEDDY ROOSEVELT

Accountability is the foundation of world-class performance in any realm. It is a critical element in your transformation and an essential step in the process of crafting the new you. To be accountable is to take ownership of all of the events, actions, and outcomes in your life. I don't mean just the good stuff that makes the highlight film, the successes and the breakthroughs, the happy moments and the positive outcomes, but your entire life: failures, disappointments, and heartbreaks included.

In case you haven't guessed, the declaration *I am accountable* is linked to the ones you made in the previous chapters. If you are aware of making every choice in your life, and if you hold that you are able to do whatever you set your mind to, then the next move is to choose to be accountable for your actions. When I am accountable, I see myself as the fundamental creative force in my life and declare that I'm unwilling to delegate this role to anyone or anything. I don't wait for any person or force outside myself to set my direction or call my shots, and I own my mistakes. I am the reason that things are the way they are.

The principle of accountability naturally grows out of the principle of choice. If you live in the declaration *I always have a choice*, then it logically follows that I am always accountable for the consequences of my choices. Like choice, accountability is an all-or-nothing proposition. You either own all of the results in your life or you cede ownership to people and forces outside of your control. And just like the declaration *I always have a choice*, the principle of accountability grants power and freedom. In this case, accountability provides freedom from blame.

To be accountable for each of my choices does not mean that I'm at fault if my choices produce undesirable results. Accountability and fault are not the same thing. Accountability means taking ownership. Fault means finger-pointing and criticizing. Whether you're berating yourself or someone else, the result is usually destructive and counterproductive. While assigning fault and blame has become one of America's favorite national pastimes—second only to whining—it is a pointless and powerless exercise. Being the generative force in my life and being at fault are mutually exclusive states.

Accountability forms the foundation for taking effective action, and that is a central component in shaping the new you: *the capacity to consistently take effective action*. Looking through the lens of accountability, my current situation can be clearly seen as nothing more or less than the collective consequence of my previous choices, not anyone else's. I assess how my choices delivered me to this point, and instead of either beating myself up or patting myself on the back, I move forward with my next choice.

Assigning fault and blame, by contrast, serves only to distract attention and produce paralysis. As we noted earlier in the book, human beings diminish and limit themselves when they fall into thinking that they made a "bad" choice, as they can't separate themselves from their choices. The same thing happens when they are held to be at fault or find themselves getting blamed for something. Rather than move into action, the tendency when being blamed for something is to defend, justify, deny, or explain the action, none of which accomplishes anything. Far too often we have witnessed people pointing their fingers at each other while a catastrophe unfolds around them. This is more than just a waste of time; it can actually have disastrous results.

In the last chapter I offered the Mercury and Apollo space programs proposed by President Kennedy back in the 1960s as models of collective ability and accountability. Those missions stand in stark contrast to our government's response to the Hurricane Katrina disaster, which was a model of dysfunction resulting from a lack of accountability. During the early hours of the 2005 disaster, when it seemed that New Orleans and its environs had been spared the worst of the hurricane, agencies were quick to claim credit for their prudence and preparedness. But when the levees broke, the Superdome filled with refugees, and the full scope of the disaster became evident, those same agencies turned on each other, denying responsibility and refusing accountability. While they were busy with the blame game, the waters kept rising, more homes were destroyed, and more lives devolved into chaos. As if this outrage weren't enough, 4 years later, much of New Orleans remains shuttered, and the bureaucratic blame game continues.

Now that we understand what happens as a result of a failure of accountability, let's talk about what happens when we are accountable. When organizations and individuals operate from the position of being accountable for the consequences of their choices, they gain a sense of power, control, effectiveness, and accomplishment.

"I choose to be accountable for my life."

Once I make this declaration, I have a new standard for assessing my actions. Are they consistent with my declaration of accountability, or are they off track? I examine each situation in a manner that illuminates how my action, or inaction, played a critical role in how things turned out as they did. In order to claim ownership and make subsequent choices as well as my next moves from a position of power, I must regard my involvement in the sequence of events, no matter how small, as pivotal. It is only from this position that I can effectively move forward. In any situation, the powerful move is to look for where my accountability lies. It is critical to remember that accountability is about the present and the future, not the past. It isn't about blaming others. It's about getting me into action.

On the other hand, if I choose not to be accountable, I choose to be a victim. The eagerness to be a victim has unfortunately reached epidemic proportions in modern America. It seems that every day we hear some new, ever-more preposterous attempt by some individual or group to claim victim status. It would be laughable if it weren't so pervasive and counterproductive.

In today's world, the declaration "I am the victim here" has become a perverse badge of honor. As you shape the new you, those are the last words that are going to come out of your mouth. Playing the victim might seem like a good way to get attention, attract sympathy, and, in the short term, get yourself off the hook for the consequences of your actions, but in the long run it renders you powerless and puts you at the mercy of people and forces outside of your control. When playing the victim, you live in the delusion of occupying some higher moral ground based on the dubious claim that you have suffered unjustly. This can be a seemingly compelling position, as you can use it to induce guilt and shame in yourself and others. However, it is not a position of authentic power. The problem with being a victim is that in the end you have to wait for someone to rescue you. Thus the victim always lives in a position of weakness. Weakness in turn breeds resentment, which eventually ferments into bitterness and cynicism. We have all seen these shrill, bitter victims of life.

"Why did this happen?" the victim demands of a world that doesn't really care about his problems. "This isn't fair," he whines, hoping that someone will change things for him. "Who was at fault, and whom can I blame?" is his response to everything. And all too often these days, the self-made victim may ask one more question: "Whom do I sue?" You can see endless variations on this theme at every turn in our daily lives.

- "My kids' grades aren't good. This has to be the teachers' fault; the public schools just aren't doing their job. Where are my vouchers for private school? Damned if I'm going to vote for that school levy."

- "My big project at work is behind schedule. It's not my fault; it's those jerks in marketing with their endless research and the bean counters in finance who won't give us the resources we need. And my boss, of course, couldn't organize a two-car funeral. It's a miracle anything gets done around here without me."

- "I keep packing on the pounds, and I never seem to have any energy. If my doctor would just do her job and prescribe the right drugs, then I wouldn't look and feel this way. And those vultures in the fast-food industry keep supersizing their portions. Following a healthy diet is just too expensive and too much trouble. And who has time to exercise?"

- "Our government is screwed up. All it does is waste my tax dollars, so why should I bother to vote or get involved in the political process? It only encourages them. Besides, I'm just one person. My vote isn't going to make any difference."

No, I haven't been reading your mind. I have just been listening to the conversations around me for years, growing increasing intolerant of this pervasive victim blather. I could quickly walk you through the examples above, showing you why these people are making themselves powerless and telling you what an accountable position would be, but I think you can figure this out for yourself by now. You also probably know how seductive the blame game is, as you see it and may unfortunately even fall into it on a daily basis. The challenge doesn't lie in seeing it in others: It is in being willing (you know that you are able) to see it in yourself, and to make a different, more powerful choice.

I do want to take a closer look at one of these examples, the whine about government: "I don't like the way elected officials operate, but I don't vote, because my vote doesn't matter." I could take this statement apart from a number of levels, but let's keep it simple for now and work with the most literal. In 2004, my home state of Washington experienced the closest gubernatorial election in American history. Following three recounts and a rancorous lawsuit, the Democratic candidate, Christine Gregoire, was declared the winner by a margin of 129 votes out of a total of some 2.5 million cast. That translates to a winning margin of 0.0045 percent, not exactly a landslide. If the number of passengers riding in a single jet had voted differently, then Gregoire's opponent would have been the winner. Now please tell me again how it is that your vote doesn't matter? Are all elections this close? No, of course not. Can any of us predict which ones will be? No, and that's the point. The victim doesn't ever want to look at his role in things. It is much easier to blame others. If you care about the way the government is or isn't functioning, then make the choice to do something about it. "But I don't know what to do," you might argue. Then make the choice to learn, to talk to someone who is doing something, find some organization that you feel an affinity with, or run for office yourself. You live in one of the few countries on the planet at the one time in history when all of these choices are available to you.

We cling to our victim stories because they are comforting and let us off the hook, not because they have genuine merit. In fact, for most people, the impulse to blame others for their difficulties has become a conditioned response: "Poor me . . . they did it to me again." By assigning fault and blame, and indulging in the fleeting but addictive pleasure of feeling sorry for yourself, you can put off the work of honestly assessing the situation and recognizing how your choices created it.

As part of the process of crafting the new you, I am going to first bring your awareness to the conditioned response of being a victim, then build your capacity to move through life living the principle of accountability. A simple way to build your accountability "muscles" is to look at any situation and ask the following simple questions:

- What's so?

- So what?

- Now what?

These three questions should be easy for you to remember, especially after we talk a bit about what each means. The power here lies in using all three of the questions in the given sequence. Victims, as you will see, get stuck on the second one and can't let it go. The easiest way to show how to use these three questions is to put ourselves into the kind of situation in which it might be tempting to operate from a "victim" mind-set, demonstrate how we can instead shift to a position of accountability, then see how much more powerful we become as a result.

Let's look at a simple example, the situation depicted in Chapter 3, "Language Shapes Reality," the classic fender-bender auto accident. We will look at it first from the point of view of being a victim and secondly from the point of view of being accountable, then use the three questions as a key to that accountability.

The situation is simple. Two cars collide at low speed in an intersection controlled by four-way stop signs. Neither driver is injured. The victim would most likely have the following experience and conversation. Upon getting out of the car, he would check to see if his vehicle was seriously damaged, then he'd go over to confront the other driver. He'd insist that he had the right-of-way, that the accident was all the other guy's fault. The other guy, also playing the victim, would try to pass the blame back to him. At this point, the first driver would get on his cell phone and either call the police to tell them he had been hit by the other driver, or call his wife and start telling her how some jerk ran the stop sign and hit his car, so it wasn't his fault he was going to be late. He would then turn his attention back to the other driver, and the volley of blame would continue until the police arrived and sorted it out. Even in the face of their assessment that he was the cause of the accident, our victim would keep protesting his innocence, accuse the officers of being incompetent or corrupt, and threaten to sue everyone involved. What a guy! As you can see, he is stuck. He isn't capable of making any assertions, only assessments, and we can clearly see that his assessments are ungrounded. His only course of action is to call the police, hoping that they will rescue him by agreeing with his version of the story. When that fails, he looks for another source of rescue: the courts.

For the accountable driver, the situation unfolds differently. His first move upon getting out of his car is to center himself, as this is the key to moving effectively in the situation. Then he moves not to check on the condition of his car but on the condition of the other driver. "Are you okay?" he might ask the other guy. "I am not sure how this happened, but let's be sure everyone is okay." Let's imagine that the second driver was another classic victim. "Oh, I'm okay all right, but you're not going to be—this is all your fault." Our accountable driver keeps his centered calm. "Well," he says, "I am sure it may seem that way, but that is hardly important now. Let's get these cars out of the intersection." He moves to do that, exchanges phone numbers with the other driver, and as the "victim" is insistent on calling the police, waits calmly for their arrival. We can see how our accountable guy approaches the situation very differently.

What's so? His car was involved in a collision with another vehicle.

So what? No one was hurt, and the damage seems minimal.

Now what? Let's move into action, clear the intersection, and let the police sort it out.

What you want to notice is that by being accountable, our second driver removes the drama from the accident. He takes ownership—not blame but ownership—for the situation. Being accountable means he operates from center, and from there he can move quickly to effective action. He isn't caught up in either generating or participating in pointless drama. Our victim will be hung up on this for weeks. He will tell all of his friends about the big wreck, limping around a bit for greater effect, and in his version he will not have been talking on his cell phone at the moment of the collision. Our accountable guy will examine things to see how his actions created this outcome, determine if and how to adjust his driving in the future, focus on getting his car fixed, and move on with his life as soon as possible.

Let's attend to that little chirping voice in your head. "Wait a minute, what about if you really are the victim? I mean, say you came to the stop sign, stopped, saw that the intersection was empty, then started to drive through only to have this other guy run the stop sign and broadside you. I mean, in that case you are the victim, aren't you?" Only if you choose to be. You can look at those circumstances and say, "There is no way that I generated this outcome. My choices were all good, and this guy was at fault." Everyone, including the cops, would agree with you, but so what? Accountability isn't about being right. It's about being powerful. Instead, I might look at this scenario and see that I chose to be out driving. I chose to take this route. I chose to stop at the sign. I chose not to look a long way down the intersecting roads. Does this make it my fault? No. But it enables me to see how my actions contributed to the outcome. That is the position of power. I am the generative force in my life, not anyone else— ever. We are all quite happy to be accountable when things are going great. "Yeah! This is my new car. You bet, I got a raise at work because I am good at what I do and that is how I could afford it. Yup, it is nice and clean because I choose to take good care of it. Oh yeah, this is all my doing. This is how I roll, baby!" There is no challenge to that form of accountability. It is the collision that tests you, not the pay raise. In fact, if you want to take this a step further, then consider this: In a truly accountable world, there is no such thing as an automobile accident. There are varying degrees of negligence but no accidents. Things don't just happen.

Accountability is a choice I make about how I am going to approach life and every situation in it. Accountability is not the same as responsibility, which can be delegated or assigned by another person; accountability occurs only by personal choice.

You will recall that earlier in the book I showed the importance of building a new and more powerful set of distinctions with which you can operate in the world. We are presently working on the distinction between accountability and responsibility. Some will argue that the terms are interchangeable, but the two phenomena are not the same. What matters here is not the label you put on the distinction, but your capacity to make and hold the distinction. Whether you decide to label this distinction accountability, responsibility, or a cheese sandwich isn't really important; what's important is that you make the distinction and choose to own the consequences of all of your actions.

Let's look at this through a work example. Imagine that your boss has given you an assignment for a major project. By virtue of the authority granted to him by his position in the organization, he can hold you responsible for completing the task in a timely, satisfactory manner. Whether or not you're accountable for your performance, however, is a choice that you make. No one else can make you accountable.

Your responsibility is measured by whether you fulfill the conditions of satisfaction for the project on time and as specified. You demonstrate your accountability by your mood while working on the project. Do you operate with enthusiasm and interest, or boredom and resentment? If you choose to be accountable, then you operate in a mood of ambition. You take ownership for making the project a success. You search for ways to deliver more than expected. Your positive mood and hustle prove contagious. Operating from accountability, you also work to ensure that your teammates are engaged and happy to be part of the project team. Following your example, your co-workers make a similar investment in their work. Rather than merely being satisfied by the project's results, your boss is delighted.

If, on the other hand, you choose not to be accountable, you work in a mood of sullen resentment. You do just enough to get by and nothing more. You poison the office atmosphere with gossip and complaints, telling anyone who will listen that the project is unworthy of your talents, that it's a waste of time and money, and that management is once again showing its incompetence. If you choose to stay in this victim mode, then you will be shocked and even more resentful when you get a bad performance review—all the more incentive to wrap yourself in the victim's dark cloak.

"After all I've done for this place," you whine, "they won't even give me a decent raise."

What the victim won't see is that he's lucky management hasn't fired him. In today's hypercompetitive business climate, "victims" are quickly left behind.

World-class teams are made up of individuals who have personally chosen to be accountable for the performance of the team. This doesn't mean that each member is individually responsible for the actions of his teammates, but that each member takes ownership for the team's collective performance. Accountability is always a personal choice; there is no such thing as team accountability.

Let me give you a very clear and powerful example of what I am pointing to. In 1984, after a long series of briefings, negotiations, and planning meetings, we, in HP2's first incarnation as Sports-Mind, secured a contract with the Army to conduct a highly classified project with the 10th Special Forces Group (SFG). The Cold War was still raging at that point, and Pentagon officials worried that the elite Soviet special forces, called *Spetsnaz*, had gained an edge over its counterpart in the U.S. military. Specifically, the generals worried that the Soviet elite forces were using the same advanced training methodologies that the Soviet-bloc athletes were using to dominate the sporting world. We were engaged to help close that perceived gap by designing a program that would match the Soviets, pushing the boundaries of human performance and better enabling our guys to accomplish their missions. To accomplish this mission, they assigned two 12-member "A" teams to us for 6 months.

After months of preparation, we traveled to Fort Devens, in Massachusetts, to begin our work. As part of the final prep work, the group's commander, Colonel Ken Getty, invited us to his headquarters for a final briefing. My team and I all had to get security clearances, and Colonel Getty informed us that what we were about to hear was highly classified.

He explained that, before starting our training program, we needed to really understand the specific nature of the 10th SFG's mission. My teammates and I glanced at each other with a bit of trepidation. We'd been talking to, working with, and even training alongside many of these operators for months, and we thought we'd had a very clear understanding of their mission. Thus we were a bit taken aback by this last-minute briefing and the tone with which it was announced. We knew that unlike the Rambo movies, real Special Forces operators spent most of their time conducting quiet, disciplined reconnaissance behind enemy lines. They lived among civilian populations, patiently gathering information and winning the locals' trust by providing medical care and engineering support.

The colonel began by telling us that the specific area of operations for the 10th SFG was Central and Eastern Europe. Their mission was to work clandestinely behind the lines in the Warsaw Pact countries, the 10th SFG operators monitored Soviet troop and weapons movements, as well as the annual Warsaw Pact maneuvers. Our Special Forces served as the nation's eyes and ears on the enemy's ground, and their coded radio reports in large part determined NATO strategy in the event that the Cold War should turn hot. None of this was big news to us. But what the colonel said next definitely caught our attention.

"So far we have been practicing the mission in countries close by and the Soviets know we are there and what we are doing. They are doing the same thing on their side as they don't want war any more than we do. But if things get hot, then the game is going to change. First of all, it will be much more difficult getting operators in, as the skies will not be friendly. We will likely lose some planes. In addition, there aren't a lot of places to hide in Central Europe. So if things turn hot, when our teams make their radio transmissions, it will be just a matter of time before the Soviets triangulate their position and hunt them down. The team won't carry much ammo with them because if they're discovered they will want to run as the odds will be very much against them in a firefight. The dilemma is that there are very few places to run to. If they make it through the Soviet troops, then they still have to make their way to an extraction point, and as the region is heavily populated, that isn't going to be easy. The bottom line," Colonel Getty concluded, "is that if things really turn hot, we don't expect more than 1 in 10 of our people to come back alive."

It took a moment for us to digest this new information. "So what you're telling us," I responded finally with a bit of a stammer, "is that you want us to train these guys for a suicide mission?"

"No," the colonel said. "I want you to give these guys everything you have, so that we maximize their chances of getting back alive."

In that moment, the entire nature of our project changed. We walked out of the briefing room clear that we needed a meeting of our own, which commenced the moment we got back to our office. The team was quiet for a few moments, and then we talked about the implications of what we had just heard. We each declared that we were in, and from there we had a conversation about what we needed to do to bring our level of play in line with what the SF operators were expecting. It was time to expand our level of accountability to match theirs.

After our meeting, we requested time with the two teams that had been assigned to us, and we asked them how they dealt with the reality that they had taken on a mission with poor survival odds. One of the sergeants explained, "Look, we are in the Army, but we're the very best in the Army, so we don't have to put up with the regular Army B.S. We get the best training there is. We get to swim and scuba dive. We ski, climb mountains, parachute, learn foreign languages, get training that would certify us as paramedics, handle exotic weapons, and blow shit up. If and when the balloon goes up, we are America's first line of defense. That's what we signed up for. So, I'm sorry, sir, what was your question again?"

That pretty much summed up the meeting. For my team, however, these mortal stakes changed the play of our game. We had a new, crystallized focus, and we pledged to bring our best every moment of every day.

Despite, or more accurately, because of, the intense and potentially violent nature of their work, the Special Forces operators refused to take themselves too seriously and developed a wry sense of humor. As part of our work with the teams, we did everything that they did and did it with them, with one exception. The Army wouldn't let us parachute, as they weren't willing to take on the liability. Most of the members of the Special Forces had gone to Ranger School, and that is where they learned to jump. The team's jump master was a character from Maine by the name of Gary Gordon. One day, during a break in training, I asked Sergeant Gordon what it would take to teach us to parachute Special Forces–style. He thought about that for just a second, smiled, and with his best Maine intonation said, "One shove, sir." This of course produced a chorus of laughter from the rest of the team and gives you a bit of insight into whom we were working with. It was also one of countless moments of friendship and bonding that we shared with these guys.

Tragically, it turned out that Gary would model accountability in a way we would never have imagined. Our training program ran for 6 extremely intense months. Afterward, we requested that the units we trained remain intact for at least a year so we could monitor their progress and assess the value of our work. Instead, after word about what we had been doing leaked out, many members of the two teams we trained were scooped up by other units. Gary Gordon and five other members were recruited into the Army's Delta Force and eventually saw action in the infamous battle in Mogadishu, Somalia, which was well depicted in the best-selling book and movie *Blackhawk Down*.

As you might recall from the book or the subsequent film, a vastly outnumbered cadre of U.S. peacekeeping troops was trapped in the city by an angry mob of Somalians after a carefully planned attempt to arrest a warlord went bad. In no time, they seemed to be fighting the entire city. A rescue helicopter that went in to help was shot down. A second helicopter flew in to rescue the downed chopper crew, and it too was shot down. Gary and Randy were on board a third chopper that was dispatched to rescue the crew of the second downed chopper. The commander in charge, having already lost two choppers, was not inclined to let them attempt a rescue. However, his concern was in direct conflict with one of the central pillars of the Special Operations world. You may have a tough time finding it written down, but a cardinal tenet of the U.S. Special Operations forces is that under no circumstances is anyone left behind. There are no exceptions to or conditions on this declaration. Their guys were on the ground, in trouble, and there was no way Gary and Randy were going to leave them there.

After being told no a number of times, they finally overcame the reluctance of their commanding officer. The two men dropped into the hot zone and immediately came under heavy fire. In short order, it became apparent that there was no way another chopper could get back in there to take them out. They fought courageously until their ammunition ran out and they were overrun. Gary Gordon and Randy Shuchart died upholding the impeccable code of honor and the principle of accountability that they lived by, and in so doing took us all to a much deeper and more profound understanding of what it meant. They were clear that they were accountable for the rescue of their fellow Americans. Not as long as it was easy, not as long as it was safe, but regardless of the circumstances, they were each accountable—period.

To summarize: In the world of victims, the game is to see how fast you can assign blame and come up with an excuse for your conduct. In the realm of accountability, the challenge is to see how far you can expand your horizon of accountability. Are you willing to be accountable for your self, your family, your company, your community, your country, your world? It may seem daunting in the beginning but remember, being accountable doesn't mean you are going to attend to everything on your own. It is an orientation to action. If you choose to be accountable for your community and believe that the parks are a mess then it may be that your first action is to pick up some trash and put it in the garbage can instead of walking by and complaining about it. That is all it takes to be accountable. Get started doing something about it. From there, you might organize a park cleanup that catches on, and the next thing you know, others are following your example. It isn't any more complex than that and you never know how others will respond to your example. It is a demanding game and one most people are unwilling to play. You now know that you have a choice.

When you choose to be accountable, every new situation becomes a challenge and an opportunity to learn. The wider you expand your horizon of accountability, the more freedom you gain from the cycle of guilt, blame, and shame that can narrow both your own life and the lives of others.

When you are being accountable, you focus on what is working rather than what is wrong.

If you choose to be a victim, then you will procrastinate, fail to meet your responsibilities, and invent elaborate excuses to explain how your failures weren't your fault.

When you're being accountable, you are always choosing, and you own the consequences of your choices.

When you are accountable, your life becomes more interesting and rewarding. You don't get caught up in pointless drama. You move through a world of your own creation with dignity and grace.

Victims tend to complain and suffer from all of life's problems. They are easily confused and frustrated. They often have an inflated sense of themselves as a defense mechanism and, curiously, seem to know everything already.

Accountable people move from center. They tend to be enthusiastic, vibrant, alive, and aware. They enjoy a sense of genuine inner peace, possess a strong self-image, and are committed to authentic learning as a way of life.

Choose accountability.

It is the only way to the new you.

ASSIGNMENT #7

FOUR SECTIONS
TIME TO COMPLETE: 7 TO 10 DAYS

SECTION #1

Accountability is a choice. No one can make or hold you accountable. Someone who has authority in a specific domain, such as
your boss at work, can hold you responsible, but only you can
make the choice and hold yourself accountable. The first part of
your assignment is to build the distinction between accountability
and responsibility.

In order to start forming the distinction between "responsibility" and "accountability," I want you to answer the following two
questions, which may seem identical but aren't:

1.   What is it that you are responsible for at work, at home, in
your community?

2.   What is it that you have chosen to be accountable for at
work, at home, in your community?

If the answer to the second question is nothing, that is fine. Be
honest with yourself. Honesty is key to accountability.

SECTION #2

When you look at the various aspects of your life, where do you see
that you are most inclined to fall into a victim story? Is there a
trend or a theme? Let's see what happens if we take a deeper look.
For the next week, make a daily accountability log. In this log, take
notes each time you find yourself falling into a victim story. It
could be a big issue or event or some simple, seemingly obscure
occurrence. Your log should have a number of entries for each day.

If you get to the end of a day and don't have anything, then you are most likely not using your awareness. At the end of the week, make some notes on what you now see about your tendency to be a victim, and share your notes with your partners if you are working with any.

SECTION #3

Let's now look in the other direction. As you have by now figured out, the new you will be accountable for everything in your life. Your assignment is to make a list of the various aspects of your life in which you intend to expand your accountability so that you can move with more power and dignity through your life. Write down:

A) The specific arenas in which you intend to increase accountability.

B) Why you've chosen to focus on those areas.

C) What being more accountable might look like.

D) How someone other than you would know that you were being more accountable.

This list ought to contain at least five items, and be sure you complete all aspects of the questions. When you have finished the list, make a final entry about how you feel after making the choice to be more accountable. When you have done all of this, share your list with your partners if you are working with any, and see what you can observe about the way they are shifting and growing.

SECTION #4

The last part of this assignment will be a bit of a stretch, and that is the point. Here is what I ask that you do. Make a short list of what you consider to be the three to five biggest issues that the country or the world is facing that you have some passion for or energy about. It could be something that you care about deeply, or something that just really annoys you to no end. For each of these issues, spend some time considering how it is that you are or can be accountable for that issue being the way it is. How have your actions contributed to the current state of affairs? When you have completed this part of the assignment, go back and, for each of the issues that bothers you, write out what it would mean to assume accountability for resolving it. That's right: What would it mean if you were to hold yourself accountable for ending world hunger, for reducing global warming, for sorting out the health-care mess? What if it were up to you: What would you do? Remember that I'm not an advocate of magical thinking. I'm not asking what you'd do if you could wave a magic wand and make it all go away. No, I mean that if it were up to you—the real you, not some fantasy you, but the new you—how would you go into action to sort things out? These issues in the world persist only because we have fallen into the trap of thinking of ourselves as victims of them and holding ourselves unable to do anything about them. You know that isn't going to sell here, so what are you going to do now?

Share your notes and insights with your partners or team, and if you are working on your own, be sure to save all of your notes, as we will come back to them.

_____

TEN

COMMITMENT

ALL GLORY COMES FROM DARING TO BEGIN.
—SHAKESPEARE

Commitment is a term that's often used and, in my view, is poorly understood. In a world where performance counts, where everything you do matters, where the smallest detail can create the difference between success and failure, commitment is everything. It is at the heart of our transformation, but exactly what is it?

We are awash in a sea of advertisements trumpeting some company or other's "commitment" to excellence, quality, customer satisfaction, going green, or global responsibility. The sports pages are filled with stories about athletes and coaches vowing commitment on the courts and playing fields. It is extolled both as a public virtue and a private character trait. Politicians wrap themselves in its cloak, lovers long to see evidence of it, and motivational speakers build careers on its value. Most people can point to the results of a commitment, or their desire for one, but miss its true nature.

A commitment is a particular type of declaration. It is the means by which we bring ourselves forth into the world. It is the move that announces to the world what it is you intend to accomplish and as such opens the possiblity for new actions for yourself and others. Critical to the nature of commitment is that it also calls forth the power of your will to achieve what you have declared yourself committed to. A commitment is a critically powerful move. It is the means by which you embody and measure your intention and focus your will. It is a key part of the process of growing yourself and developing your competence. It is therefore fundamental to the development of the new you and central to your transformation. Action begins when you make the declaration, "I am committed to . . . " Before this statement, there is only possibility; afterward, there is certainty.

Despite the basic nature of this principle, most people struggle with it. They wonder what it is they are committed to, doubt their capacity really to commit to anything or anyone, or dither about when and how to go about doing it. While understandable, this anxiety is pointless. Here is the deal: There is no such thing as a life without commitment. You have already made and are living out a host of commitments, whether or not you are aware of it. Thus the question to consider is not *Am I committed?* It is *What am I committed to?* To find the answer to this question, you have only to look around you. What you are committed to is revealed in what you have produced or failed to produce. Look at the life you have created, and you will see exactly what it is you are committed to. There is no more accurate standard of the measure of your commitment.

When it comes down to it, as you may remember from our discussion of the nature of the mind, most people are committed to looking good, being right, and playing it safe. Your incapacity to achieve or realize the things you say you want, the things that you claim will make you happier and more satisfied, is due in part to your attachment to looking good, being right, and playing it safe, and in part to the fact that you think a commitment is merely an idea, a product of the mind. That isn't the case. A real commitment is a powerful somatic declaration, not simply a function of the mind but of your entire being.

For instance, imagine you need to lose weight but you're having trouble doing so. You might say: "I am really committed to losing weight, but this exercise and healthy-eating program isn't working for me." I would argue that you're not truly committed to losing weight. You are committed to looking good, which in this case means telling your friends and family you're trying to lose weight. You are committed to being right, because you are deeply attached to the story you have sold yourself, that diets don't work for you. To really commit to losing weight would mean having to let go of your story. You are committed to playing it safe, as evidenced by your halfhearted stabs at all of the fad exercise programs and diets. This is much safer than running the risk of the genuine success or failure that would come from fully committing yourself to the task. Although it may sound harsh, all evidence points to the fact that you're committed to remaining overweight, to talking about losing weight rather than doing it, and to feeling sorry for yourself, declaring yourself a victim of your genes or some other force comfortably beyond your control, rather than taking charge. You are committed to maintaining your present size and shape, because at some level it makes you feel safe.

How can I be so insensitive and uncaring? By this point in our process, I'm sure you've realized that I am not going to sugarcoat things for you. I care about you, and that's why I insist upon being straight with you. The ones who don't care are your so-called friends who continue to listen to your story, all the while knowing it is complete bunk, and smile and agree about how hard life is, and how unfortunate you are, then quietly watch you eat another cheeseburger with fries. They are more committed to playing it safe than to taking care of you, which in this case means making you realize that you do have the power to change in any way you want to. The fact is that the person who struggles with extra pounds can lose weight. While genetics plays a part in determining our body type and shape, there is no one who is incapable of changing his diet and exercise patterns to achieve great results. The key is committing to making this happen and being accountable for your commitment.

Let's look at another example of a person who believes that he has made a commitment to something but doesn't like the results. Consider the parent who says, "I am really committed to being a good parent, but my kids refuse to listen to me and they keep getting in trouble." Again, notice the desire to blame, to not be accountable. These principles—choice, accountability, and commitment—are all inextricably linked. As a parent myself, I know that raising a child can be tough. To be clear, there are no right or wrong answers here, no absolutes in terms of the best way to go about doing something, but there are choices and consequences, and the results of these choices are the ultimate measure of commitment, so they speak for themselves.

I've learned the hard way that my commitment to being the best parent I can be to my 12-year-old daughter, Cheyenne, doesn't mean doing everything for her or giving her everything that she wants. While giving in to her every desire may be easier in the moment, being a good parent frequently means doing the opposite: doing things she doesn't like, want, or agree with, and entering uncomfortable conversations. It also means making time for things that I might not want to do. It means putting up with the rolled eyes and occasional, "But Dad, all the other kids get to . . . "

Let me give you an example. Last summer, Cheyenne and I were visiting my friend Joel, who, in addition to being a member of our management team, spends some of his weekends working with horses in a nature preserve. He asked her if she would like to ride one, and Cheyenne, who had been taking riding lessons, enthusiastically accepted. We saddled up one of the horses, and Cheyenne climbed on. Holding a lead rope, I walked the horse up the trail.

After a few minutes, I turned to see that Joel was about 50 yards behind us. Because she was looking comfortable, I asked Cheyenne if she wanted to ride back to Joel on her own. She nodded. I tied the lead rope loosely around the saddle horn and called out to Joel to let him know that Cheyenne was heading his way. She had ridden only a few yards, however, when her horse stepped on a dried branch, which shattered and jabbed its leg. This spooked the horse, and he bolted.

It became immediately clear that Cheyenne's riding lessons had not prepared her for this moment. She could not stop the horse, which ran past Joel and threw her from the saddle. Sprinting toward the tall, wet grass in which she'd landed, I logged my fastest 50-yard dash in years. Cheyenne was shaken, crying, and frightened, but uninjured. While Joel retrieved the horse, I checked for signs of a concussion or any broken bones. After she had calmed down a bit, I got her to her feet. We walked around for a few minutes to be sure she was okay, and then I encouraged her to get back on the horse.

Cheyenne, of course, didn't want to get near the animal. But I explained that both she and the horse would learn the wrong kind of lesson if she didn't climb back into the saddle. At that moment, Cheyenne didn't like or agree with me. However, reluctantly, she did as I asked. I walked the horse around by the lead rope for several minutes, and she gradually stopped feeling afraid. And in the months since the incident, her story has shifted from, "Dad made me get back on the horse," to, "I fell off the horse but I brushed myself off and got right back on." Her self-confidence and self-esteem have risen as a result. For my part, I'm glad that I held my commitment to doing what was best in the long term for my daughter and didn't give in to doing what was easiest in the moment.

Let's consider another common example. Frustrated with the fact that you keep getting passed over for promotions at work, you might say: "I'm really committed to getting promoted at the office, but nothing I do seems to be working."

Are you really? Let's examine this statement. You say you're committed to this goal, but did you have a conversation with your boss and ask her specifically what it would take for you to earn a promotion? Did you conduct a grounded self-assessment of your skills and job performance, and compare them with those of your co-workers? Did you make a concrete, detailed plan to improve your job performance? Did you look beyond your company to determine how you stacked up against others in your industry? If the answer to any of these questions is no, then you might discover that what has been passing as a commitment was actually an expectation, and a false one. "Well, I've been here for 4 years. Isn't that long enough to expect a promotion?" Not necessarily.

Today's economic environment is so competitive that merely being present and putting in your time isn't nearly enough. Your competition is no longer national, but global. People all over the world want your job. If you have not yet responded to this new reality, then now is a good time to start.

I know that I'm being a bit rough on you, but I've been watching what is going on in India, China, and Brazil, and we all need to wake up. I'm not trying to make you feel afraid or panicked, just aware of the changing world around you and your place in it. For a long time, we in America have prided ourselves on the competence and creativity of our workforce and banked on our capacity to maintain the world's highest living standards. But we can no longer take our competitive advantage for granted, as it is rapidly eroding. We can no longer coast on our reputation or mistake expectations for commitments. It is time to get back to making the kind of bold commitments that made us great in the first place. That's right: I am envisioning a new America, peopled with individuals just like you.

Recently, I gave a 3-hour presentation at a management institute in Delhi, India. After my talk, students and local CEOs eagerly grilled me with questions for another 2 hours. They would have stayed hours longer if the head of the institute hadn't finally sent them home. I have rarely, if ever, seen a similar level of commitment to learning among American business students and business leaders.

Like it or not, we are living in a new world, and in this new world, performance is what matters. By performance, I mean your capacity to generate results, to show up as you intend, as a worker, wife, sister, husband, son, friend, brother, listener, or parent. In this interconnected, hypercompetitive world, *commitment means doing whatever it takes to produce the desired result*. It means putting every bit of yourself into the task at hand. You must commit all of your energy, intelligence, and passion to generate what you have declared you will produce. Commitment begins with the linguistic move of a declaration, but it can't stop there. It must also live in the realm of action. A simple formula exists for remembering this:

COMMITMENT + ACTION = RESULTS

While the above formula is very simple, bringing it consistently to life can pose some problems. To help you avoid needless suffering and self-doubt, let's spend a bit of time looking at some typical beginner's mistakes.

Many people fail to see the distinction between doing everything they already know and doing whatever it takes to achieve the result they committed to.

For example, let's say that you want to have a better relationship with your wife. The two of you don't seem to be communicating well, and there is a growing distance between you. You have always said that you were committed to your marriage, and now you decide to put your commitment into action and throw yourself into the challenge. You make a point of asking her more about her day when you both get home. You set aside more time to be together, go out to dinner at least once a week, but after 3 weeks, none of this seems to be making any difference. In fact, things seem even worse. In the face of your perceived failure, it is easy to doubt yourself, to beat yourself up, or to interpret the lack of desired results as a sign that you're not committed to your goal. But is this really the case? Maybe the ways you already know for enhancing your relationship aren't the ones you need to produce the intended result. This is the moment in which you need to use your awareness and make some grounded assessments about the situation.

Are you truly committed to having a better marriage? If the authentic answer is yes, then go to the next question. Have you given this commitment your best effort? If the answer is again yes, that brings us to the point: Sometimes doing everything you know how to do does not produce the desired result. This is the moment in which doing everything you know is not what it takes. Commitment means doing whatever it takes, not just what you know how to do, but whatever it takes. In these instances, if you are truly committed and doing what you know how to do isn't producing the result, then get some help, support, coaching, or training to help you achieve that result. If you are committed to having a better marriage, then this commitment must trump your commitments to looking good, being right, and playing it safe. There is nothing to be ashamed of, embarrassed by, or mad about. In fact, it ought to be a relief: You can ask for and accept help by granting yourself access to the resources of the world.

In this case, you decide to call a marriage counselor and schedule an appointment. In the course of your first conversation, you discover that while your wife very much appreciated your efforts to improve communication and spend more time together, she was growing increasingly annoyed by the way you missed her signals that what she really wanted was for you to pay more attention to your sex life. Her signals were subtle, and you missed them because you were so fixated on doing what you knew how to do. In this particular case, fixing the problem would be not only simple but also fun.

People often make the mistake of thinking that true commitment can be anything less than 100 percent. For the new you, there is no such thing as being sort-of, kind-of, or mostly committed. It is all or nothing: You are either in or out; there are no gray areas here. Thinking that you can hedge your bets, keep all your options open, or get by with something less than your best is a nonstarter. To the adolescent mind, commitment often looks like a loss of freedom: "If I commit to this person/this career/this place, then I am giving up my freedom to make other choices." Trapped inside this mind-set, you could analyze, fantasize, and otherwise fritter away years while keeping your perceived options open. Instead, life is passing you by. Failing to make a commitment, you dissipate your energies instead of focusing them.

In the ancient days, it was a common practice for an invading army to literally burn their boats after landing on a foreign shore, thus closing off any possibility of retreat. They were then 100 percent committed to the upcoming battle, as there was no means of escape, no back door. This is the metaphorical move that you need to be willing to make with yourself. Many people think that if they are involved with something or someone for an extended period of time, then it shows their commitment. Not so. Commitment isn't about the time you spend. It is that moment in which you close all of your back doors, say no to the other options, stop shopping for new possibilities, and devote your entire being to whatever it is you have committed to.

Here is why I insist that there are no gray areas. If you claim to be 90 percent committed, then the remaining 10 percent serves as a breeding ground for excuses and for nonperformance. Your area of noncommitment might be small, but it is always big enough to get you off the hook. By not being all the way in, you have left yourself a way out, and that is not a position of true power. True power comes from accountability, from accepting that you choose everything in your life, and from owning those choices. All of this adds up to commitment.

By the same token, if you merely declare that you're going to "try" to reach a goal, or "maybe" complete an assignment, then you won't accomplish either one. What do you suppose would have happened in the 1960s, for example, if President Kennedy had challenged America to "try" to put a man on the moon within 10 years? That single, three-letter word would have given him political cover for failure and also provided NASA and the aerospace industry excuses for corporate and bureaucratic foot-dragging. Given their immensity and complexity, anything less than total commitment would certainly have sunk the Mercury and Apollo projects.

Fortunately, like all great leaders, President Kennedy understood the all-or-nothing nature of commitment. By refusing to grant America room to make excuses, he made it possible for the nation to accomplish an amazing goal. In fact, the now-famous phrase "failure is not an option" was first voiced by the NASA mission controller as his team was working to salvage the stricken Apollo 13 mission.

Here are a few simple adages that you can use to help you understand the principle of commitment and how to bring it to your life:

- When I am unclear about my commitment, I procrastinate. When I am clear about my commitment, I act.

- When I am unclear about my commitment, I talk about doing my job. When I am clear about my commitment, I do my job.

- When I am unclear about my commitment, I maintain my image. When I am clear about my commitment, I maintain my integrity.

- When I am unclear about my commitment, I play to look good. When I am clear about my commitment, I play so everyone feels like a winner.

- When I am unclear about my commitment, I am confused and full of doubt. When I am clear about my commitment, my intention is focused and my actions are on purpose.

We are living in an increasingly demanding world, and if you intend to take your place in this world, then it is imperative that you learn to make and hold commitments. Reduced to its simplest and essential core, the new you that we are building is nothing more than an amalgam of your commitments. The new you makes commitments consciously, chooses them clearly, and is accountable for bringing them to life.

ASSIGNMENT #8

FIVE SECTIONS
TIME TO COMPLETE: 2 TO 3 WEEKS

SECTION #1

As I said earlier, commitment isn't about the time you spend; it's about a line you cross with yourself. To bring this claim to life, let's begin with another inventory. Use your awareness and make a list of the parts of your life where you are now clear you have been putting in time as opposed to truly being committed. This could be your job, some "friendships," different relationships, workout programs, diets; it doesn't matter. What matters is that you drive yourself to be aware of where in your life you have been just going through the motions. It may take a few sittings to have a complete list, and if there aren't at least 10 entries, you aren't done, so stay with it until you are.

SECTION #2

Once you have the list, let's make some choices. Going through the motions is no way to spend your life. It won't bring about your transformation, and it is certainly not the way the new you is going to choose to live. Are you going to be committed to the items on the list? If so, what new actions do you need to take? If not, what do you see that you need to do to either complete or clean up the situation? By when in the next 2 weeks will you take these actions? Make clear commitments to action and include timelines. Once you have completed all of the actions, make an inventory of what is now different, what it is you are clear you are committed to, and how you feel as a result. Put some detail into all of these notes. As usual, if you are working with a team or a partner, share your notes on all of this. If you would like some help with some of this, go to the Web site and you will find a template that you can use to take you through the process.

SECTION #3

Let's take a deeper cut at this. You have been at this process of inventing a new you for a while, so by now you ought to have a sense of how the new you will be configured. What new commitments do you see that you need to make if you are going to craft a new future for yourself? Again, make a list of these new commitments. Then go another step: What results do you see that you will produce as the measure of your commitment? Be specific about the what and the when. Take two or three items off the list and work them through to completion. I realize that the time lag between commitment and completion could be days or weeks. Regardless of how long it takes to complete these items, once you do, make some notes about what you now see regarding what it means to be committed and how it feels to go from commitment to action to results.

SECTION #4

Here is a special little gift for you. Based on all the blather that has been generated on the topic I am about to touch on, this could likely be a book on its own, but because you have stayed committed to your learning to this point, I want to give it to you in simple form. One of the big complaints that I hear everywhere today is that "I don't have enough time." Everyone, everywhere lives in a story called "I am too busy." At work this goes a step further, with more ominous consequences, and becomes a pervasive mood that we call *overwhelm*. This is a story people fall into in which there is too much to do, too much to know, not enough time, and not enough resources—and it isn't ever going to change.

Our collective response to this mess has been endless sets of tips and techniques for what has been termed *time management*. To put it simply, this is all largely useless B.S. As usual, this is a solution that is focused on the symptom, not the cause. To find the resolution to this dilemma, we need to get at the root cause.

The issue has little to do with time or its management. It isn't as if we have somehow lately been running short of time. There are still 24 hours in a day, and this is likely to continue into the foreseeable future. Thus the issue isn't time management; it's commitment management. When we aren't clear about what we are committed to, we tend to get overinvolved, and this is what produces the mess in question. Involvement and commitment are not the same thing, and this is a key distinction. A lack of clear commitments opens the door to the tendency to say yes to too much and no to not enough. Combine this with a universal tendency to overestimate our capacity, and we have all the makings of the current mess.

The way out is simple. Become very clear about your commitments and rank them. Do this and watch what happens. Make a list of the three to five topmost commitments in your life. For example, let's say you are committed to being a good parent. You know that I will tell you this is too vague, so let's go another step. What sub-commitments can you articulate under what I am going to call the umbrella intention of being a good parent? "I am going to spend three nights a week with my kids. That means from the time I get home until they are doing their homework or are in bed." Reach that level of detail with each of your three to five commitments. When you have your list together, the next step is to rank the commitments. Force yourself to decide which is number one and which is number five. Your mind will want to waffle and tell you they are all equally important. No, they aren't; your mind is just being lazy. If they were all equally important, then I suggest that none of them are all that important, and you need a new list. It is time to be rigorous with yourself. Here is your test. You have just been told by your doctor that you have 24 hours to live. Which of the things on your list would you attend to? You have time for only one, so which is it? That should help clarify your priorities. If your answer is "none of them," then you need to rework the list.

When you are done with the list, pull out your calendar for the last 2 weeks and see how your allocation of time aligns with your commitments.

The next step will be a bit of a challenge, but you should be counting on that by now. In my experience, a human being can't carry more than five to seven authentic commitments. We simply don't have the capacity to attend to more than that. This is where you need to make the distinction between what you are committed to and what you are involved in. It is time to drop some of your involvements and shore up your commitments. Yes, people may be disappointed, but this is about changing yourself, not them. Take a week or so to reallocate your time so that it is in alignment with your commitments. When you have done that, make some notes about what you have cut from your schedule, how you have readjusted your allocation of time to align with your commitments, and most importantly, how you feel as a result.

SECTION #5

You are now well past the halfway point in our process. It is therefore time for a bit of reflection. Take some notes about what you assess you've learned so far. How are you shifting and growing? How do you see your world changing? What new possibilities do you see for yourself? What do you see about your willingness and capacity for commitment, and the role this is going to play in shaping your new future?

As always, share your notes with your partners and have a conversation about what you have learned in the process. If you are working alone, keep your notes for the future.

ELEVEN

TRUST

> WE MUST WALK CONSCIOUSLY ONLY PART WAY
> TOWARD OUR GOAL AND THEN LEAP IN THE DARK TO
> OUR SUCCESS.
> —HENRY DAVID THOREAU

Trust is the bedrock that all relationships are built on. It is the essential element that holds together a winning team, whether in business, sports, or the military. It is the key to nurturing family relationships, productive business relationships, satisfying friendships, and, ultimately, flourishing societies. By the same token, where there is a fundamental lack of trust, relationships aren't sustainable and teams fall apart. I claim that our incapacity to build and rebuild trust is at the root of much of the trouble in our society today.

Why is this important to us in the process of your transformation? Because human beings are inherently social animals, we exist in the context of our interactions with each other. If you intend to make a positive difference in the world as an individual and as a member of a team, then you must first develop a new interpretation of trust, one that opens new possibilities for action. This means you must let go of your old conception of trust, just as earlier in this process you let go of your preconceived notions about language and learning. Without forging a new interpretation of trust, you'll be forced to call on your default, "common sense" definition of it, and it is this same "common sense" that is failing us on an increasingly grand scale.

If we were to ask most people what trust is, they would respond by providing a host of examples.

- "Trust means knowing you can count on someone when the chips are down."
- "Trust is being able to share your deepest feelings with someone."
- "Trust means knowing that you're not going to be hurt or betrayed."
- "Trust is when they go to you for the shot at the buzzer."

This is a list that could go on for some time, and while we can all probably come up with additional examples of trusting behavior, none of them really answers the question: What is trust? These attributes or anecdotes describe what trust looks like, the situations in which it is likely to show up, and how people feel when they are trusted or trusting. What they haven't done is answer the fundamental question. What is trust?

If we press our inquiry further, we will most likely get past the attributes and anecdotes and find that the common understanding of trust is that it is a "feeling" you have, or some "thing" that must be earned. This is the unexamined, default definition that we are going to take issue with, examine in detail, and replace with something more precise and powerful.

Let's begin by examining the notion that trust is a "feeling." Feelings and emotions are, of course, a fundamental and important aspect of being human. While they have tremendous, often overwhelming power, feelings are at the same time notoriously mercurial. They are subject to change without notice. As we all know, any number of variables can affect my feelings. "The sun is shining this morning, so I feel cheerful and optimistic." "I've got a nasty cold and I barely slept last night, so I am feeling cranky." "My husband and I had an argument this morning, and all day I've been feeling blue."

These shifts of feeling, dependent on external factors, are normal, natural, and an expected part of life. But if feelings come and go, shaped by external factors, are they the solid foundation upon which you want to build your relationships? Do you want to think of trust the same way you think about the weather? When it comes to the weather, the only thing I can count on with certainty is that it will change, and I have no capacity to affect it. I live at the mercy of the weather, just as most people live at the mercy of their feelings. This is not a path of power, nor the way to shaping the new you.

Please be clear: I am not saying you ought not to have feelings, nor that you should ignore them. I am instead suggesting that when it comes to trust, the most fundamental element of all your relationships, including the one with yourself, you should build on a more solid foundation.

The other default definition of trust holds that it is an object or a thing. You can see this in the way people discuss it. "I gave him my trust, but he broke it," says a woman about her boyfriend. "I had to take it back, and now he'll have to earn it all over again." It's as if trust were a glass, a bike, or an iPhone, something to be borrowed, lent, bestowed, and generally passed around. Of course, in reality, we all know trust isn't a tangible thing. What you might not realize is that holding trust to be an object robs a person of power and thrusts him into the role of victim.

Look at the above statement again: "I gave him my trust, but he broke it. Now he'll have to earn it all over again." Who is moving from a position of power in this interaction? Is it the woman whose trust has been betrayed, or the man whom she claims to be untrustworthy? It is the man who has the power, because the woman has ceded ownership of the situation and is holding herself as a victim. Even though the woman seems to be the powerful actor by claiming to take her trust back, the man drives this action. In this common narrative, it is up to the man to "earn back" the woman's trust. It may seem like she retains some power or control, because she is granting and withholding trust. However, she cedes to the man the final authority of earning, holding, and, if he so chooses, again squandering her trust. This is not an authentic position of power for the woman.

Let's review: So far I have told you that trust is the glue that binds all of our relationships, be they personal or professional. Nothing revolutionary there. From there, I suggested that our default definitions of trust, which hold that it is a feeling or a thing, are extremely limiting and thus not at all powerful. Now it is time to take a new view on trust, to form a clearer distinction of what it is, and to figure out how to get that real glue to bind your relationships from now on so that they consistently hold together.

I propose a more potent interpretation of trust, one that is consistent with and constructed from your new set of basic linguistic moves. Rather than regarding trust as a feeling or an object, I hold that *trust is an assessment I make about someone when he or she commits to taking a specific action.* The action could be as simple as showing up for a lunch date on time, meeting a deadline at work, or stepping into the lineup when a starter gets hurt. In this interpretation, feelings are left out of the equation and trust is de-objectified. Instead, a person's actions are assessed against three distinct standards: *sincerity, competence,* and *reliability.*

Sincerity means that you are being honest with me. If you are being sincere with me, then you are not holding back some part of your truth or conducting your own private, internal conversation that is different from the one we are sharing. You are not telling me one thing and another person something else about our interactions and agreements.

Competence means that you are able to perform the actions necessary to fulfill a commitment. Where we get ourselves in trouble in this regard is when we confuse a lack of competence with a lack of sincerity. If I promise to produce a report for you, to do my best work, and what I turn in is woefully inadequate, that doesn't necessarily mean that I was insincere when I said I would do it. It more likely means that I am not yet competent to do the level of work that you require.

Reliability means that you have a history of fulfilling your commitments on time and as promised. The mechanic who over the years consistently repairs cars and gets them done when he says he would will be assessed by his customers as reliable, and his business will thrive. The basketball player who throughout every game of the season takes the shots in clutch situations, hustles after loose balls, plays consistently intense defense, and gives 100 percent during practice will be assessed as reliable by his coach and teammates, and will be seen as a role model by new players. If I consistently deliver well-researched and clearly written reports by agreed-upon deadlines, then my boss will assess me as a reliable employee and reward me accordingly.

The assessment of trust is yours to make about me and mine to make about you. You can't "give" me sincerity, competence, or reliability, and the quality of trust that comes as a result of these three things isn't mine to "win" or "lose." My sincerity, competence, and reliability can be assessed only by other people, and they do that based on the actions I take and the conversations I engage in. I do the same with others.

One of the big problems in many workplaces today is that too many people overpromise and underdeliver. They say yes to everything and are not competent at assessing their capacity or negotiating for time and resources. The net effect of this is that we live in a constant state of being overwhelmed, which fuels assessments about our lack of competence.

This breakdown is driven not as much by malicious intent as by

fear and the desire to please. People are afraid to say no or to negotiate with their bosses. But as a result, it becomes hard to trust
them when they say they have what it takes to get a job done. For
instance, I was recently talking to a landscaper who had done some
work around my house about the need for a new well. Initially he
suggested that his crew could do the work, but after a few conversations it became clear to me that they were not competent to get
the job done. He wasn't maliciously trying to deceive me. He was
sincere—he wanted the job and believed he could do it—but there
were simply no grounds for the assessment that he was competent.
He had never done a well project before, and he lacked the equip-
ment, training, and proper licenses to do the job. This doesn't mean
I won't trust him to continue landscaping for me. It just means he
isn't competent in the realm of digging wells.

Why do these distinctions among sincerity, competence, and
reliability matter? Because each separate assessment drives different choices and actions, and shapes my ongoing relationships. A
breakdown in the realm of sincerity will be treated very differently than a breakdown in the realm of competence and it is very
critical to be able to make these distinctions.

I can say, for example, that I trust my osteopath to take care of
my ailing knee. I have assessed that he is sincere in his declared
commitment to practice medicine; he has completed many years
of rigorous education and acquired a license. I have assessed that
he is competent, as he has passed a battery of examinations and
peer reviews to be board certified in his specialty of osteopathy. I
assess that he is reliable because he has a long history of doing
what he says he will do when he says he will do it. In addition, he
doesn't keep people waiting in his office, and he is well regarded
in our community and the smaller medical community as being
someone we can rely on. Based on this three-part assessment, I
trust him to take care of my body.

However, I may not trust him to fix my car. There is no evidence whatsoever to suggest that he knows a fuel injector from an alternator. Just like competence, trust is an assessment, and it is domain specific. Like it or not, others generate these assessments about us based on the actions that we take. This brings us back to the point I made early in the book, in the chapter on linguistic moves. We are not the stories we tell ourselves about ourselves. We are the sum of the assessments of our actions, as viewed by others. If you are consistently on time to work, if you act in a reliable manner, then people will begin to view you as timely and reliable, and you will be timely and reliable. This is an assessment, sure, but it's more grounded than any story your inner cynic might have been whispering in your head.

Why is all of this so important? Because if you fail to carefully distinguish the three assessments of trust, you are likely to collapse them into a single blanket assessment, generating a chain of misguided choices and undesired consequences. For example, I might fall into the trap of assessing a person as insincere if she does not fulfill a commitment to me, when in fact she was not competent to do so. Let's say that a new friend offered to pick me up from the airport, then failed to show up at the designated time. I might make the mistaken assumption that she "flaked" or didn't care enough about me to honor her promise, when in fact she wasn't familiar with the highway system and became lost en route to the airport. If you do not hone your distinctions of trust, you lose your capacity to take appropriate actions.

Confusing sincerity, competence, and reliability often produces misunderstandings and leads to mistaken assessments in the workplace. These in turn lead to damaged relationships and underwhelming performance. For example, let's say that a sales manager for a large publishing company fails to deliver his team's quarterly report to his boss on the day he promised it would be ready. The boss may subsequently assess him as insincere, the knee-jerk response to a lack of performance. "I can't trust that guy," he thinks to himself. But the sales manager was utterly sincere when he promised to get the report in. He wanted to please his boss and fully intended to meet the deadline. He simply promised more than he could reasonably and realistically deliver. What he suffered from was a lack not of sincerity but of competence, in both compiling the report and in managing his commitments.

Unfortunately, because his boss doesn't have the capacity to make these distinctions when it comes to trust, he is going to collapse them together into a single assessment of distrust, with potentially dire consequences for our poor manager. Most people don't make these crucial distinctions when it comes to trust, and when they say they don't trust someone, they are most often calling that person insincere, often unjustly. In our society, an assessment of distrust or insincerity carries an intensely negative moral judgment. When we hear someone say, "You can't trust that guy Harry," we don't interpret that to mean he might not be competent in some domain. We interpret that to mean that the person has some moral or character flaw. We tend to segregate individuals we judge as morally defective into a box, and regardless of how that person acts in the future, he is likely to remain in that box forever. In this case, once Harry's boss assesses that he doesn't trust him, i.e., thinks he is insincere, Harry had better start sending out his resume.

While you might not like to think of yourself as incompetent, the assessment of a lack of competence does not carry the same heavy moral baggage as being insincere. After all, we don't expect other people to be competent in every realm, not without training or coaching or guidance of some kind. The good news about a lack of competence is that it can always be remedied. It's not a character flaw, just a learning gap. As you saw in our conversation about learning, given the time, resources, and commitment, virtually anybody can become competent in virtually any endeavor. We can teach this manager how to negotiate with his boss. We can teach him how to manage his commitments and even the nonfulfillment of them.

A lack of sincerity, by contrast, looms as a character flaw. For example, if he didn't get the report done on time because he was found to be spending the afternoon on the golf course, his boss could reasonably ground an assessment of insincerity, and the intelligent move would be to stop dealing with the person. There is little chance that you can change another person's level of sincerity, and you can almost guarantee that if someone displayed a lack of sincerity once, he will do so again and again.

On a brighter note, it's important to realize that distinctions of trust are dynamic; they can shift according to the actions that people take. If you gain competence in a realm where you previously lacked it, and people see evidence of this, then they can start to trust you where before they didn't.

The power in this new interpretation is that it affords you a new world of choices and frees you from the limitations of the current default definitions of trust. Trust isn't a feeling, and it isn't a thing. It is a dynamic set of assessments that you make when someone promises to take some action. If you can bring these distinctions to life by becoming more aware of the nature of the assessments you make when you say that you do or do not trust someone, then you will be able to move in entirely new ways to build and sustain powerful relationships in all aspects of your life. The capacity to assess, build, rebuild, and sustain trust is essential for the new you.

ASSIGNMENT #9

THREE SECTIONS
TIME TO COMPLETE: 1 TO 2 WEEKS

SECTION #1

Let's begin by doing some work on honing the distinctions of trust and making them operational in your life. Make a list of five people in your life (past or present) with whom you have some trust issues. Maybe you are just uneasy around them, or find that your gut instinct is that you're not inclined to trust them. For each of the people on your list, identify which of the three (or which combination of the three) trust assessments you hold of the person. When that is complete, go one more step and ground each assessment. In other words, for each assessment you make, answer the question, "Why do you say that about him/her?" When you have completed this, make some notes on what this project revealed to you. What did you see about your historical way of holding trust and the people in question? What possibilities does this new distinction of trust open for you?

SECTION #2

Let's now move from the other direction: outside in. Make a new list, this time of people who you believe have trust issues with you. Hopefully the list will not be too long, but it ought to have at least three to five people on it. After all, none of us are perfect. When you have this list complete, make some notes on why it is that each person in question might have trust issues with you. "He is a jerk" isn't the answer I am looking for. Instead, note whatever it is that may have happened between you two, and then look again through your new distinctions of trust. What do you now see about how your behavior or choices were interpreted or assessed? Which assessment of you might the other person be living with, and how does it compare with your assessment of yourself? Again, take notes on what this exercise reveals to you, then make some comments on what new possibilities open up out of this inquiry.

SECTION #3

What I have intended so far is for you to break out of your historical understanding of trust and achieve the freedom that comes with a new, more powerful view. So that we can see how well your outcome aligns with this intention, do the following: Over the next week, keep a log of incidents in which you see the distinctions of trust come alive. Remember that the assessment is relevant and comes to life only when someone makes a promise to you. In your log, make at least three to five notations, every day, of promises that others make to you. They don't have to be big ones. Did your assistant leave the mail on your desk as promised? Did your spouse remember to buy milk so that you could have it with your coffee in the morning? For each promise, note what your initial assessment of trust is for the person making the promise. Do you hold them as sincere, competent, and reliable, or do you have some concern in one of the domains? Make notes and provide grounding for the areas of concern. If you assess that the person is sincere, competent, and reliable, provide grounding for this as well. At the end of the week, review your log and take some notes on what you now see about trust, what new possibilities are opening for you, what new actions you intend to take, and how you see that these new distinctions can reshape your future.

As always, if you are working with partners, share your notes and thoughts about all of this. If not, save your notes as we will come back to them.

HONESTY

In the last chapter, I made the claim that trust is the glue that binds all of our relationships, be they business or personal. I then went on to say that the traditional "common sense" interpretation of trust, that it is a feeling or a thing, is very limiting. I explained that if you intend to move through life with dignity, grace, and power, then you need to develop a new interpretation of trust. I proposed a new view in which trust is an assessment that you generate when someone makes a promise to you. You assess the person's trustworthiness based upon his or her sincerity, competence, and reliability.

Of these three qualities, we established that sincerity is the most important, because in our society we regard sincerity as a measure of character. While focused training can remedy a lack of competence or reliability, if people view you as insincere—if your actions have led them to believe that you don't really intend to honor your promises—this is harder to fix. As a result of your transformation, the new you needs to develop the capacity to build and rebuild trust. What this means is learning how to act—and therefore generate the assessment of being sincere.

On the surface, the process is simple. If you want others to assess you as sincere, then be sincere; when you make promises, fulfill them. Be honest and straight with people. Being honest is the fundamental means by which you evoke the trust of your friends, family, teammates, co-workers, and customers. And as we have seen, without trust there is no chance that the new you can emerge or that your team can rise to a level of world-class performance. It is therefore essential that you embody the practice of honesty. Again, that sounds easy enough. But what exactly does it mean to be honest?

The common definition of honesty is "telling the truth." When we were children, we were immersed in this version of honesty like guppies in water. Our parents told us "Honesty is the best policy." They rewarded us for telling the truth, and punished us for telling lies. The virtue of honesty was drummed into us by the legend of the young George Washington chopping down the unfortunate cherry tree, a story that turned out to be a myth. But like most myths it came with a message, and as a result almost every American child learned the famous words, "I cannot tell a lie."

Our society holds truthfulness to be one of its core values, and virtually everyone assumes that he or she knows what it means to tell the truth. But as you might by now expect, I am once again going to challenge this conventional wisdom, the default definition, and provide you with a more refined set of distinctions with which to operate in the world. Let me begin by offering the notion that telling the truth is not quite as simple as it may seem. Let's start by examining the nature of the truth itself. Instead of holding it as some single, monolithic absolute, I propose that there are actually three kinds of truth.

First there is THE TRUTH, which is interpreted as universal, absolute, and unquestionable. This is the truth that is generally associated with religion. This type of truth stems from belief and faith. The established religions of the world are all based on this type of truth. Too often, unfortunately, followers of the various religious traditions are convinced of the divine, inviolate, unassailable correctness of their truth, and their truth becomes the basis for righteousness. Unfortunately, as we all know, this type of righteousness has been the source of unspeakable acts of cruelty throughout history.

The second type of truth is what we can call The Truth. In this category we find universally observable phenomena, verifiable facts, and those matters and occurrences that can accurately be labeled as true and false. This is the realm of mathematics and the hard sciences, where we use accepted practices for observing, interpreting, and crafting the assertions that we call the truth. In this world of truth, $2 + 2 = 4$, grass is green, the sky is blue, water is wet, and rocks are hard. Most people on the planet would agree that all of these statements are true. In terms of our linguistic moves, this is where assertions can be found.

Finally we come to the third type of truth, which we refer to as My Truth. My truth consists of my experiences, my interpretations, my memories, my thoughts, my feelings, my sensations, my state of being, my beliefs, and my assessments. This vast category typically encompasses much of what people are referring to when they talk about "telling the truth."

These distinctions are critical to your transformation, as trouble arises when you confuse My Truth with the other two kinds. In fact, I can make the claim that most of the conflict and suffering on the planet stems from the failure to distinguish among these categories of truth. Combine this lack of rigorous distinction with the fact that human beings are the only living creatures willing, and often eager, to fight and die for the sake of "the truth," and you have the recipe for the violent hash we have made of much of the world. Equipped with a more accurate and powerful set of distinctions, the new you can avoid this tragic confusion. By escaping the trap of collapsing the three categories of truth into one, moreover, you can help others reach more peaceful and productive outcomes.

To reach that point, you must first deepen your awareness of what constitutes your own version of My Truth. The degree to which you are aware is the degree to which you are willing to let yourself know your own truth. This practice begins with centering, as there is no possibility of deepening self-awareness without returning to your center, which is your foundation. Starting from center allows you to hone your capacity to listen to the deeper communications that are present within you all the time.

For instance, many people get bollixed up thinking that they will get into trouble if they are really honest and tell the truth. A classic example of this error of thinking occurs in the workplace: "I can't tell my boss what I really think of him," you convince yourself. "If I did, I'd get fired." On the contrary, you're more likely to get into trouble by not telling enough truth, first to yourself and then to your boss. Let me show you what I am pointing you to.

Let's say that, like countless employees in offices and workplaces all around the world, you think your boss is a jerk. Of course, expressing this opinion to him might not be a career-enhancing move. You would understandably find yourself in a mess; however, it's not because you're telling the truth, but because you're not telling enough of the truth. To understand what I mean by this, let's take a closer look at the situation.

Remember, this is about your degree of self-awareness. In this moment, all you are aware of are your feelings—which we established in the last chapter are as changeable and uncontrollable as the weather—and your feeling is that you are frustrated, and the tendency is to dodge accountability by blaming it on your boss. Thus, your boss is a jerk. If you go a little deeper, however, and ask yourself the next question, something else might show up. Imagine that you and I are having a conversation about your jerky boss.

"Why do you say your boss is a jerk?" I ask.

"Well, he never acknowledges my good work," you reply. "I turn in projects on time, I get good performance reviews, and my customers love me, but I never hear anything about it from him."

"So that means he's a jerk?"

"Yes!"

"All right," I say. "So your boss doesn't acknowledge your work. What do you think that means?"

"It means he's a jerk."

"I'm pretty clear that's how you feel," I say. "But I want you to probe that feeling. What do you think it means about how he regards you?"

"He obviously doesn't think I'm very important," you say. "He doesn't value what I do."

"All right, you believe that your boss doesn't hold you as important. Can you see the possibility that the reason you're so bothered by this perception is that you have your own doubts about your importance?"

"What do you mean?"

"It's simple, really. In part, the reason this bothers you so much is that you have your own lingering doubts about your importance to the company. When your boss fails to acknowledge you as you think he should, it triggers those doubts. Rather than face and examine these doubts, you get angry and direct your anger outward to your boss, who becomes a jerk."

This hypothetical exchange may strike you as a piece of armchair psychology, but I intend it to show how you can use your awareness to reach a deeper truth. If you were to go with your initial feeling and tell your boss that he's a jerk or, even worse, if you ridiculed him as a jerk behind his back with your co-workers, you may very well find yourself unemployed, and deservedly so.

If, on the other hand, you took a moment to use your awareness, the situation could unfold differently. You could request a meeting with your boss during which you might tell him that it is your experience (My Truth) that he doesn't recognize your work. You go on to say that what happens when you don't feel recognized is that you worry about your value to the organization. Moreover, this worry is chipping away at your loyalty to the company. Moving from this level of awareness and accountability (notice there is no blame in this conversation) and opening with this deeper truth, you could have a much less dramatic, much more honest, and much more constructive conversation. This is a conversation that any boss would be able to hear, and one that is much more likely to enhance the way your boss views you and to lead to the recognition you are seeking. Clearly this would be a much more powerful move than telling him, "You're a jerk!" Instead of jeopardizing your career by telling a surface version of the truth, you have enhanced your career by revealing a deeper truth.

As you can see, telling the truth is not quite as simple as it might seem. The first step is to learn to distinguish between the three types of truth. "Jesus is Lord," "Allah is all knowing," "The way of the Buddha is the way to peace" are all THE TRUTH, inside of their respective belief systems. It is when any of the practitioners of these belief systems attempt to impose their version of THE TRUTH on others that we have trouble. Two plus two equals four, rocks are hard, grass is green, the sky is blue: All are The Truth. Anyone, anywhere on the planet, would agree with them. "My boss is a jerk" is a version of My Truth, which offers a limited and subjective version of my reality. "My boss's lack of recognition for my efforts is triggering me to worry about my place in the company" is a much deeper and more authentic version of My Truth—a truth that can be communicated without creating damage. Once you learn to recognize the sort of truth you are telling, you can then become more rigorous about how you hold the truth and the way in which you communicate it. There is nothing right and therefore nothing to be righteous about when it comes to My Truth, and My Truth forms the vast majority of our human communication. Learning these distinctions enables you to both listen to and speak "truth" much more powerfully. Once you have developed competence with these distinctions of truth, you can then move into the practice of honesty, which in turn has its own set of distinctions.

LYING: I INTENTIONALLY TELL YOU SOMETHING I KNOW TO BE FALSE.

WITHHOLDING: I CHOOSE NOT TO TELL YOU SOMETHING THAT I AM AWARE OF.

HONESTY: I CHOOSE TO TELL YOU ALL OF THE TRUTH THAT I AM AWARE OF.

While it is true that some people lie on a regular basis, most of us are more likely to withhold. What this means is that we tell some but not all of the truth. We can always find a way to rationalize this practice: "I don't want to hurt someone's feelings." "I don't want to make a scene." "I don't want to get into trouble," and so on. A supposed concern for another person provides a seemingly viable basis for these excuses for why we don't tell the whole truth. If I'm willing to probe more deeply, however, I will frequently find that my concern isn't really someone else's feelings, but rather my unwillingness to cope with another's reactions to hearing my truth. In fact, it's not the other person's feelings I'm concerned with, but my own. While you may not have developed competence in this regard, there are ways to tell your truth so that the person you're speaking to doesn't feel attacked and is able to hear you and understand your needs and point of view.

For example, let's say that you feel disrespected by a manager at work. The first step is to remember that this is your assessment. It is not The Truth but it is Your Truth. And there is a way that you can engage this manager and speak your truth so that he might be able to listen to you without feeling ambushed and agree to change his behavior.

The next step is to have a conversation with the person in question. To be done properly, this conversation needs to be live and in person, not via e-mail or on the phone. Set a specific time for the conversation. This isn't something that you are going to just happen to do the next time you see this manager in the hall or as part of some larger conversation or event. Tell him that the reason you would like to speak to him is that you are concerned about an issue between the two of you that you would like to resolve. Once you sit down at the designated time and place, center yourself, take a breath, and move into the conversation by being 100 percent accountable for things being the way they are. There is no room for blaming, finger-pointing, or fault-finding. You completely own the situation.

"Hi Joe," you might begin by saying to your manager, "I appreciate your willingness to sit down with me and work through this issue that has been bothering me. Here is what is on my mind. In our marketing meetings, I often find myself feeling that you do not respect me. I know this isn't your intention, so please let me explain. When we go to the meetings in the boardroom, it is my experience that you always sit at the head of the table, put me at the far end, don't call on me when I raise my hand for questions, and don't distribute the reports that I produce. I know you don't mean to ignore me or to generate these feelings."

What you want to notice here is that the speaker in the above paragraph is taking accountability for the situation, beginning statements with the small but crucial word "I": "I appreciate"/"I feel"/"it is my experience." No blame is being cast upon Joe. No one is attacking him; rather, you are spelling out Your Truth. After this is done, you can continue recounting your experience, or you can go to the part that matters. You have covered "what's so" and "so what," and it's time to get to "now what." You state your request. "At the next meeting, I would like to sit at your right hand, distribute my report, and be called on during the question periods. Is that something you can agree to?"

This conversation will produce a very different result than one that starts with: "Joe, you are an arrogant jerk, and I am tired of the way you treat me with disrespect during our marketing meetings!" While this accusation would likely result in your getting fired, any reasonable person could listen to your "I" statements without feeling assaulted. Moreover, if you are centered while you speak your truth, you will likely find that Joe agrees with at least part of your request. And you've managed to speak your whole truth, without withholding anything.

Withholding might seem like a good strategy to spare trouble in the short run, but in the long run it is typically a recipe for disaster. Here is why. If you think about it, more often than not, you know when someone is withholding from you. After some conversations, you experience the vague but unmistakable somatic sensation that something isn't quite right. You have that lingering sense that something isn't being told to you. Your mind starts racing. It is addicted to coherence. It wants things to make sense, and it can't deal well with chaos and randomness. Thus, when you get that somatic sensation that someone isn't being straight with you, your mind goes to work making up a story about what this withholding means. The problem is that your mind tends to be a drama queen, and the stories it makes up are often catastrophic. This is a mental practice that we call catastrophising.

For example, a young man shows up at his girlfriend's house to take her out to dinner. At the door he asks how she is, and she replies, "Fine," while shooting him what he interprets to be a cool look. Triggered by this terse reply and the look that accompanied it, his mind takes off at a gallop. "Oh my gawd. There's something she isn't telling me. She is really pissed at me. How can that be? What did I do? How can I fix it? I know, I'll buy her some flowers . . . no!

Some candy . . . " All of this drama and angst is revealed to be for naught when she finally reports that she's annoyed because in spite of all of her hard work, she saw that once again, his tie clashed with his shirt. This is Her Truth, not The Truth, but she might have spared him a lot of stress if she hadn't withheld it, just as he might have spared himself had he simply asked her what was up rather than letting his mind catastrophise on him.

My point here is that more often than not you know when someone is withholding something from you. This is good news. The rest of the news is that other people know when you are withholding something from them, too. This is part of our human hardwiring. Don't be so naive as to think that you are the only one who can tell when you're hearing only part of the truth.

Not only is the mind prone to catastrophising like a drama queen, but it also has another very effective self-sabotaging trick. In this case what I am pointing to is that as soon as the mind makes up one of these catastrophic stories, the very next thing it does is forget that it just made the story up. Instead, in an instant, the mind transforms the story it fabricated, and it becomes The Truth. This adds a lot of unnecessary drama to your life, and it hurts the chances that any sort of partnership will succeed.

If I have any intention of building trust, which is the bedrock of solid relationships, then I must be willing to be honest. If I cannot trust my friends, my family, or my teammates, I am left in a state of not knowing. If I don't know, then I worry, and when I worry, my mind invents explanations, meanings, and stories about the situation. In an environment where everyone is busy inventing his or her own catastrophic version of everything, the possibility of trust evaporates in a haze of rumor, gossip, innuendo, and guarded conversation.

Being honest isn't always easy. But I want to know the truth, and I infer from this desire that others also want and deserve the same thing. Being honest requires consistent courage and a commitment to being accountable. You can use this simple rule of thumb as a guideline: *If there is some doubt as to whether or not you should communicate something to another person, then you should.* If whatever the "it" is, is in the way of your working or relating, then you need to have the conversation. Often the question of whether or not to communicate is itself getting in the way of your working or being with that person, and inhibiting your relationship. Thus the resolution is to communicate. At the same time it is important to be clear that this guideline is to be applied only to things that are "in the way" of your working or relating. This isn't a license to pile all of your emotional junk on everyone. If Your Truth is that you don't like Joe's tie and that is in the way of your working together, then you need to consider working at home and leaving Joe alone. If something that trivial is bothering you to the point that you have trouble working with Joe, then you need to take a deeper look at yourself and find out what is really going on. I am working with you to build an expanded version of you, not a diminished, nitpicky version.

There are risks in being honest. If you don't use your awareness and you blurt out your initial truth without thinking about how you want to phrase it, you may upset people. You need to take the time to figure out what Your Truth is and how you can phrase it in "I" statements so that you're staying accountable and not simply attacking or blaming the other person.

Finally, much as I may not like it, not everyone wants to hear the truth. Thus, for those who lack courage, it's always tempting to play the "you first" game: "I will be honest with you, but you be honest with me first." "I will when you will." Honesty, however, is not a game, and playing "you first" is neither accountable nor a potent strategy. It is far more powerful to choose to be first, to take the risk, and set the standard. This is where you need to bring your courage and commitment to your transformation and to shaping your new world.

ASSIGNMENT #10

THREE SECTIONS
TIME TO COMPLETE: 1 WEEK

SECTION #1

Honesty is a topic that triggers a lot of controversy and dispute. In part, I suggest, this is due to the fact that most people do not have useful distinctions about it. You are now well equipped to move in a new way in the world.

As noted in the first part of the chapter, honesty is the means by which we generate the assessment of sincerity. The practice consists of the seemingly simple process of telling the truth. What I revealed to you was that there are three types of truth, and you get into trouble when you confuse My Truth with the other two. With that in mind, let's start with a bit of awareness work. Over the next 3 days, make a point of reading your favorite publications, be they newspapers or magazines, and making some notes on what you see about how the three types of truth show up, and when and how you see them get confused, either intentionally or otherwise. Make some notes in which you cite specific examples and point them out to your partners, if you're working in a group.

SECTION #2

The next task is to learn a new practice that I am going to call accountable communication. This is the key to being able to tell Your Truth without unnecessarily offending others. The practice begins with deepening your awareness. To do this, I am going to ask that you go to the Web site and look under assignment #10. There you will find a grid that will walk you through the process of deepening your awareness. Take some time to make your way through the grid; the process is simple and, with the guidance provided, it ought to be easy.

Use this new practice as a means of working through issues or breakdowns that you've had with at least five people. Work each of the issues or breakdowns down to the fifth level of awareness, then make some notes on what was revealed to you about this particular person and the real source of the breakdown. Make some additional notes on what you are now beginning to see about what it means to be accountable both in general and in terms of communication.

SECTION #3

Look back at the example I provided in this chapter, where I show how you might ask a manager, Joe, for a sit-down and phrase your feelings in powerful "I" statements, concluding with clear examples for what you'd like to see change. Think of someone in your life with whom you have an issue you'd like to resolve, and ask him or her to sit down, face-to-face, to talk it out with you. Plan the "I" statements you're going to make to this person ahead of time. Speak your truth and don't withhold anything important. Practice the conversation a few times in the mirror or with your partners. When you are ready, go and engage. Afterward, make some detailed notes on how the conversation unfolded, what the outcome was, and what your mood is now that you have completed it. Make some additional notes on what you now see about the practice of honesty, the utility of accountable communication, and the possibilities that these practices open for you as you look at your future.

As always, share your notes and engage in conversations with your partners. If you are working solo, save your notes as we will review them.

THIRTEEN

INTEGRITY

> AS HUMAN BEINGS, OUR GREATNESS LIES NOT SO
> MUCH IN BEING ABLE TO REMAKE THE WORLD AS IN
> BEING ABLE TO REMAKE OURSELVES.
> —GANDHI

In last chapter's conversation on honesty, I said that being honest isn't always easy. If it were easy, it wouldn't be such an uncommon practice. Instead we saw that most people either withhold portions of their truth or wait for others to be the first to take the risk of being honest. The risk, in this case, is that others may have a negative reaction to hearing your truth. In this chapter, I am going to show you how, in the end, the reward for being honest far outweighs the risk.

The practice of honesty is central to the final performance principle we are going to work on: integrity. As we near the end of our work, it is time to start bringing together the building blocks of the new you that we have assembled thus far. The focus of this chapter is integrity. It is crucial to our task, as integrity is what holds these building blocks together. Let's begin with a look at the fundamental structure of integrity, then move toward making it operational.

In the process of becoming an adult, you have developed a set of personal values. This is the code by which you live. You began to develop this code early in life, and it is an amalgam of beliefs, teaching, philosophy, and role-modeling that came from a variety of sources. Consciously or unconsciously, you emulated certain values of your parents, or, if you found their values unpalatable, you may have attempted to live your life in direct opposition to the way they lived theirs.

After your parents, your experiences in school helped shape your values, exposing you to people outside of your immediate family and friends and their beliefs. Your formative role models probably included characters from movies and TV shows, books, and other media. Churches and other community organizations contributed to your value system, as did your peers. In summary, all of your interactions with the world have contributed to the formation of your value system. Your unique combination of experience, education, and inculcation led you to this point and gave you the yardstick by which you measure your actions and those of others. What does all of this have to do with integrity? Everything!

Our English word *integrity* derives from the Latin root word *integer*, which means oneness or wholeness. My interpretation of integrity stems from this root meaning. In the world that the new you inhabits, *integrity means achieving unity of thought, word, and action*. As has been the case with many of the other principles we have explored and worked on, we must assess integrity on a binary scale. You are either "in" or "out" of integrity. You can't have "a little" integrity. It's an all-or-nothing proposition.

When I say that I am "in integrity," it means that what I say is consistent with what I think, and what I do is consistent with what I say and think. At that point I have achieved a unity and am literally one in all three realms. When I am in integrity, I experience the inner sense of oneness or wholeness that comes from living by my personal code. When I am in integrity, I am at peace with myself because I am living my values. I build my integrity through my actions and by engaging in conversations that are coherent and consistent with my thoughts and values. When I am in integrity, I carry myself in the world with a sense of well-earned dignity.

Most people believe that integrity is a positive value, but in keeping with this new interpretation I hold that integrity is value neutral. Unfortunately there are any number of vile people who live in integrity; their thoughts, words, and actions are all consistently vile. It may well be my assessment that these people have bankrupt or morally deficient value systems, and while my assessment may be grounded, it is just my assessment, my truth. Much as we may not like it, these people are in integrity. Thus while there is a connection between your values and your integrity, they are not cut from the same cloth. Integrity is not a value. It is a measure of the degree to which I live my values.

Life offers us all an endless series of opportunities to test our integrity. Most of these tests are small, have minor consequences, and may go by unnoticed. However, it is often in these small, seemingly insignificant moments that our integrity is found lacking. You know what I am talking about. You say you believe in being honest, but then withhold your truth from your wife, maybe about something small, like the price of the stereo you bought. "It's no big deal," you say. "She isn't always straight with me. I know those new shoes cost more than she let on. We both do it all the time." You may not see this as a test of integrity, yet it serves that function nonetheless. You tell your kids to stay away from drugs, but you come home from work every night and light up a cigarette and open a bottle of wine. "That isn't the same thing as doing drugs," you protest. "This can't be what you mean by an integrity test!" Yes, I'm afraid it is.

One of your declared values at work is treating all people with dignity and respect, but you remain silent when a colleague tells blatantly racist jokes. "Oh come on, everyone laughed at it and no one was hurt by it," you rationalize. "Lighten up and quit being so freaking PC. This doesn't have anything to do with integrity." Yes, actually, it does.

While these examples may seem small and easy to let slide by, sometimes life sends you a test via special delivery that is too big to be ignored. For example, I claim that I believe in being honest and am committed to the well-being of the people with whom I work. Given that, what do I do when I learn that a safety violation is being covered up at work? Do I keep my mouth shut because I don't want to jeopardize my job, or do I take the risk of annoying senior management by speaking up?

I believe that children should be protected from abusers. What do I do when I see a woman shaking and hitting a child in a parking lot? Do I intervene to stop her, or do I get into my car and mind my own business, while rationalizing that the woman must be the child's mother and I don't know the circumstances well enough to intervene?

I claim to believe in our company's vision. I know that what we do provides a valuable service in the world. So when I hear some co-workers cynically disparaging it and our leaders over lunch, do I say something to defend the company or pretend I didn't hear and keep eating my sandwich?

In each of these cases, I have a choice. Some of my choices will keep me in integrity, while others will take me out of integrity. It is vital that I remain aware of how my choices affect my integrity and of how my integrity in turn affects my total being. When I am out of integrity, I diminish my dignity and my self-respect suffers. I constantly judge and doubt myself and experience inner turmoil and discord. If left unchecked, this internal strife will manifest itself physically and eventually compromise my immune system. I know that may seem a bit far-fetched, but this connection between our mental and emotional states and our physical condition has been unequivocally proven by ongoing research in the emerging medical science of psychoneuroimmunology.

Let me bring this down to earth for you by sharing a simple personal story with which I suspect many of you will be able to identify. Some years ago, as I moved into my late twenties, I found myself feeling increasingly listless and apathetic. I didn't seem to have much energy and was tired a lot of the time. I found that my range of emotional responses narrowed as well. Nothing much got me excited and nothing much got me upset. I couldn't seem to muster either the interest or the passion to care deeply about anything or anyone. For a while I actually thought I was sick, so I went to the doctor to get a physical and was somewhat surprised to find that I was in perfect health.

I then had a flash of misguided insight, as it occurred to me that what I was experiencing—the physical, mental, and emotional stupor—was simply what happened when you started getting "old." Like everyone in his or her twenties, I thought I was immortal, and I was horrified by my conclusion that I was already experiencing the symptoms of aging. After all, only "really old" people were supposed to suffer from a decrease in vitality and passion, not someone in the prime of life. Lucky for me, a wise teacher helped me to see that what I was experiencing was not the result of getting "old" but rather the cumulative effect of living a life that was, in large part, out of integrity.

Let me take you on a metaphorical boat ride, to show you what I was experiencing and what you may be experiencing too. For the sake of this story, let's assume that life is an ocean, and the tides and waves represent the endless set of challenges and possibilities that life has to offer. Your birthright is the opportunity to sail these seas, to battle with the tides, to find your way over and across the waves, and to experience the richness that this ocean of life has to offer. To sail these often-stormy seas of life, you need a sturdy, seaworthy craft. For this journey, your fine sailing boat is built from your values. These are the spars and planks that shape your boat. The vessel's key component, the one that enables it to grab hold of the wind and skim across the sea, is the sail. On your boat, this sail is your integrity. In this case it is a fine, gossamer sail that sparkles in the sun.

As we discussed earlier, the sea of life is constantly churning with opportunities for you, the sailor, to test your integrity. Every time you fail one of these tests, the effect is that you poke a hole in your sail. That's right: Every time you say "yes" and do "no," tell another little white lie, or sell yourself out by doing what you know is contrary to your values, you poke a hole in your sail. If you aren't aware and you continue acting out of integrity, one day you will find that your grand adventure has come to a halt because you have more holes than sail. That was exactly the condition that I found myself in years ago. My lack of passion, energy, caring, or involvement had nothing to do with getting older and everything to do with having sold out my values. I was out of integrity.

To be clear, I hadn't gone over to the dark side or anything. It wasn't as if I was sticking up the 7-Eleven or selling crack in the schoolyard. However, the cumulative effect of an ongoing series of little acts of both commission and omission was deadening. I was stuck in a relationship that wasn't particularly satisfying, more out of inertia than love. I had a vague sense that I was supposed to be doing something of significance with my life, but I couldn't figure out what it was, so I was essentially treading water in a series of small jobs that didn't challenge me. As you learned earlier, I had been a campus political activist and had carried that passion for change out of college and into the world. But after watching a series of political candidates for whom I had worked fail to make their promised changes, I had fallen into resignation and turned my back on what I saw as the whole corrupt mess. I went through the motions of having a good time and enjoying life, but at some deep level I knew that I was just going through the motions. The net effect was that my body was alive, but I felt dead. Slowly but surely, day after aimless day, even though I was unaware of it, I was doing my best to kill my spirit.

How did I get myself out of this mess? How was I able to get my becalmed boat back under sail? Here comes some more good news. This fine gossamer sail that is your integrity is not like any regular fabric. Like the rest of you, it is dynamic and alive. You can repair all of the holes in your integrity by bringing yourself back into alignment, by getting back in integrity. That's right, just stop selling out. No more saying "yes" when you mean "no." No more taking the easy way out, turning a blind eye, pretending you didn't see or hear something that bothered you. You get your self and your life back by living in integrity.

In my case, this meant that I told the truth about my relationship both to myself and to my partner, and we agreed it was time to go our separate ways. No more pretending. I took a professional risk by turning down unchallenging jobs and starting the first iteration of the Human Potential Project. I retired from rugby and turned my attention to aikido and growing the new business. I cleaned up a host of little messes I had made that ranged from long-standing debts to dangling, incomplete communications. The net effect was that I suddenly felt alive again in my early thirties in a way that I had not in my late twenties.

Right about now, your little inner cynic may be sounding off. "That's nice for him, but I am doing fine. There isn't that much that I need to attend to." Or: "It can't be as simple as he is making it sound. There must be something more to this." The very basic truth is that you don't need any more help than what I just offered. With this chapter, I am giving you the same gift that my teacher gave to me years ago. If my story of feeling dead on the inside is speaking to you at some level, reminding you of a similar period in your own life—perhaps even this very moment—then take comfort in the fact that you too have what it takes to get back in integrity and reclaim your birthright to enjoy the journey of life.

If you want a simple test that will roughly but accurately gauge how you are doing, try this. Before you go to bed tonight, stand in front of a mirror and recount for yourself the current condition of your life. Talk about how your work is going and how satisfied you are with it. Talk about your relationships with family, friends, and co-workers. Talk about your connection to and with spirit in your life. Talk about your physical well-being and how you are doing at taking care of your body. Talk about the things that evoke your passion, that make you excited. Talk about the aspects of life that arouse your anger and indignation. Don't skip any of these conversations, and make it a point to look yourself in the eye while you are doing your recounting. If you find that there is a moment when you have a tough time forcing yourself to keep eye contact, then that is a good indicator that you have found an aspect of life where you are out of integrity in some way.

You should by now know what to do with this awareness. That's right: Make a choice to take a new or different action that will clean up the messes, big or little, that you have made in this area, and commit yourself to this new action. From there you move with accountability to get yourself back in integrity. It won't take long before you find that your vitality is back.

Integrity is so powerful because it builds on itself. The more consistent you are in your thoughts, words, and actions, the easier it becomes to be true to yourself, and the more complete you feel. With that as the foundation, let's complete the conversation about honesty.

Even for the new you, there will be moments when living this principle of honesty will seem particularly challenging. You will ask yourself why you can't let it slide, just this once. Your inner cynic will howl that it is too much work, or that right at this moment, the potential payoff is just not worth the effort. These are the occasions when you center yourself and remember this conversation is about integrity.

What it comes down to is this. You know that you can fool everyone else into believing that you are in integrity, but you can't fool yourself. Regardless of how difficult it may be in some moments to maintain your integrity, I promise you it is much easier than contending with the feeling you have when you don't really want to make eye contact with that person looking back at you in the mirror. I live these universal performance principles, including the principle of honesty, in spite of the fact that it isn't easy. I don't do it for other people. I do it for me. It is a divine selfishness that drives me. In the end, I am less concerned about what others think than what I think of myself. I live a new life, in unity with all of these principles, because to do anything less would be out of integrity, and I am unwilling to pay that price. What is your choice?

Here are a few bullet points for you to use as you navigate the seas of life:

- You are in integrity when you keep agreements, when people can count on you to do what you say you are going to do. You are out of integrity when you break agreements, when you begin things and don't complete them, when you promise and don't deliver, and when you say "yes" when you mean "no" or when you say "yes" and do "no."

- You are in integrity when you listen to your body and take good care of yourself—mentally, physically, and spiritually. You are out of integrity when you do things that undermine your health and well-being.

- In the course of your life, you will have a host of opportunities to reflect on your choices and how they line up with your values. If you are afraid of what you might see, you will keep yourself constantly busy. You will make sure that there is never any time to feel the impact of your choices and their consequences. This addiction to being busy is a sad but all-too-common practice in our society, one that eventually leads to a deadening of the spirit and a pervasive lethargy. You may want to explain this away as just a part of growing up and getting older. It doesn't have to be this way. You can wake up and make another choice.

Maintaining your integrity will not always be easy. You may risk disapproval, unpopularity, and the threat of confrontation. The rewards will be self-respect, dignity, clarity, and the inner peace that comes from being true to your values.

ASSIGNMENT #11

FIVE SECTIONS
TIME TO COMPLETE: 1 WEEK PLUS
IMPLEMENTATION TIME

SECTION #1

You may find this assignment a bit tough to complete and rough on the ego. I am certain it will send your inner cynic into fits of denial and defensiveness. All of that is to be expected. Your job is to stay true to your commitment to seeing your transformation through to completion, build a new you, and stick with the process. We are very near the end, so deepen your commitment and sprint to the finish.

Let's begin with the process of articulating your code. While most of us have a general sense of what we believe in, you will find that there is much power in finely honing and declaring your values. The process is simple. Begin by writing a list of the values, principles, and beliefs that you hold most strongly.

- I believe in being honest.
- I hold that it is important for me to be debt free.
- I believe I am accountable for the financial well-being of my family.
- I value my physical well-being and, while not concerned about getting old, I want to take care of my body as well as I can.
- I believe in being a lifelong learner.

These are all examples of what I am pointing to. Take what may be vague notions about what you hold to be important and craft them into a clear set of declarations. You will find that this process may unfold over a few sittings, and you will find that things come to you after a bit of reflection. Make an initial list and then let it rest. Come back in a day or so, reread what you have, then see what is missing. You should have at least 10 statements on the list. As a final aspect to this part of the assignment, make some notes on what you saw about yourself as you went through the process. Pay attention to how you felt when you started, how your inner cynic worked to interfere, and how you feel now that the assignment is complete.

SECTION #2

In the next step, do the exercise I detailed above in which you give yourself a report on the current status of your life while standing in front of a mirror. The entire report should take at least 3 minutes, preferably longer. You will find that this is initially very awkward, and that is okay. Make a report on all of the aspects of your life: your health, financial well-being, relationships, career, hobbies, politics, spiritual life, education, and so on. When you have completed this report, take some notes on what you experienced as you were doing the practice. Your inner cynic will chime in with, "I felt like a dork doing this. Are you happy now?" Ignore that critical voice and go deeper into your somatic self for a more genuine answer. The goal is to produce an inventory of the aspects of life in which you are clear you are out of integrity. This means the parts of life in which what you are currently doing is not in alignment with the values you declared above. Your list should have at least 5 to 10 items on it. If not, you are most likely deluding yourself, so stay with it. They don't have to be big issues, so wake up to the subtleties of how you are living your life and write them down. Include in your notes some comments about what you observe in terms of your emotional state as you make this list. Are you embarrassed, ashamed, annoyed at me for making you do this? Whatever you are experiencing, use your awareness to explore the feeling or emotion and write it down.

SECTION #3

When you have your list, the next step is to begin the process of restoring your integrity by determining how you are going to get yourself back "in." The answer will, of course, depend on what you have on your list. For each item on your list, write out what it is you see that you are going to do to restore yourself to integrity. It may be that you have to stop taking some actions, clean up relationships, fulfill long-overdue promises, or simply declare that the promise is not going to be fulfilled and apologize to the person to whom you made the promise. Work on your list until you have a resolution for each of the areas in which you are out of integrity.

For example, let's say that one of your self-declared values is to attend to the financial future of your family. This means staying current on your monthly bills, putting away some money for retirement, and ensuring that you have a rainy-day fund in case of some emergency. You know all of this, but instead of doing these actions you bought a new car and a new boat, and you're planning a series of vacations. This would be an example of being out of integrity. What is the action to take? Cancel the vacations, put the money into investments that are easily liquidated, and set yourself a timeline for getting the IRA and rainy-day funds up to appropriate levels.

Go into this level of detail with each and every one of the items on your list. When you have completed your action plan, including dates for achieving each goal, make a new set of notes about what you have observed in this process. What was your mind doing? How did the inner cynic show up? How do you feel now?

SECTION #4

The next step is pretty obvious: Put your plan into action. Start with a few of the simple items, the ones that you can clean up quickly, so you get some momentum. Be sure to acknowledge each completion and commend yourself as you make your way through your list. From here I can't say how long this should take, but if it is more than a month or so, you are either procrastinating or you have some pretty complex messes to sort out. Don't let your inner cynic sabotage you here: Stay with it and get it all done, regardless of how long it takes.

SECTION #5

Now that you cleaned up the messes you made in the past, your next step is to attend to the future. In this part of the assignment I want you to spend some time reflecting on what you went through in the process of cleaning up your integrity. I hope you came to the same realization that I did, which is that while living by your values may at times be challenging, it is much easier than dealing with the realization that you have sold yourself out. With that as the background, make one final list. On this list, note the new declarations that you are going to make to help you live your life by your values. What new actions do you commit yourself to taking? What historical actions are you going to quit doing? How are you going to reallocate your time, energy, and finances? When you have completed this list, print it out, and put it someplace visible so that you will see it on a regular basis. The bathroom mirror is a good spot, as is the refrigerator. It doesn't matter where you put it; what matters is that it stays put where you can see it.

As you now know, the final step is to share your notes and observations about the process with your partners or teammates. Again, if you are working alone, keep your notes, as we will come back to them, very soon now!

FOURTEEN

BEING A STAND

> IT IS FROM THE NUMBERLESS DIVERSE ACTS OF
> COURAGE AND BELIEF THAT HUMAN HISTORY IS
> SHAPED. EACH TIME A MAN STANDS UP FOR AN
> IDEAL, OR ACTS TO IMPROVE THE LOT OF OTHERS,
> OR STRIKES OUT AGAINST INJUSTICE, HE SENDS
> A TINY RIPPLE OF HOPE, AND CROSSING EACH
> OTHER FROM A MILLION DIFFERENT CENTERS OF
> ENERGY AND DARING THOSE RIPPLES BUILD A
> CURRENT WHICH CAN SWEEP DOWN THE
> MIGHTIEST WALLS OF OPPRESSION AND
> RESISTANCE.
> —ROBERT F. KENNEDY

Congratulations! You have now reached the final stage in our work together. By making it this far, you've proven your commitment to learning, to seeing your transformation through to completion, to crafting the new you, and to designing a new future for yourself. This is no small accomplishment, and I acknowledge you for your commitment and effort. What I have done so far is give you all of the pieces that you need to accomplish your bold and ambitious goals. Now it is time to put these pieces together to complete your transformation and craft a new, more powerful unity: a new you.

In this final chapter, we are going to set our sights on tackling the age-old question: "What is the meaning of my life?" This may seem like a curiously ambitious departure from the work we have done to date, but everything we have moved through so far has been preparation for this, the capstone of the process. While the question of the meaning of life has been the source of debate for ages, we are joining the inquiry at an interesting historical moment. As a society, we enjoy greater prosperity, better health, longer lives, more freedom, and a vastly wider range of choices than any other people in history. We are better educated, possess more knowledge about our world, enjoy an unprecedented capacity for communication, and have broader possibilities for our lives than ever before. Yet at the same time we are more discontented, disoriented, unsatisfied, unfulfilled, dispassionate, disconnected, and uninvolved. I believe that this suffering is a result of failing in the quest for meaning in our lives.

I won't pretend to be able to resolve this quandary for you in an instant—or perhaps even at all. What I am going to do is take you through a process that will help you resolve this central dilemma of being human. My goal is to help you clarify what you believe in and ultimately stand for in life. In the new world you are poised to step into, a *stand* is a deep, life-shaping declaration. It is the declaration that announces to the world what it is you care about and what you dedicate your life to. Why is this important? Because *being a stand* for something is essential in your quest to achieve power, dignity, clarity, focus, satisfaction, and, ultimately, meaning in life.

Before we go further, I want to offer you a brief explanatory note. As you have now come to see, everything that I am working on with you is designed to shift your way of being in the world. I am not much interested in what you understand, whether you can repeat verbatim everything you've read, or whatever new terms you might have learned. What I care about is who you have become and who you are as a result of the work that you have done. When I use the phrase "being a stand," my editor cringes a bit, as it isn't a grammatically proper construction, but it is exactly what I mean. I am not talking about thinking about a stand, debating a stand, or even shaping, taking, or holding a stand. Those are all one step removed from the genuine power that lies in embodying your stand, in having it be alive in every fiber of your body. That is what I mean when I say "being a stand." So while acknowledging that I am breaking a grammatical rule, I am going to move into a conversation about building and being authentic power in the world.

The purpose of these notes and the accompanying reflective writing assignment is to help you clarify what you stand for in life. Our claim is that being a stand for something is essential to your capacity to have power, dignity, clarity, focus, and satisfaction in life. Throughout history, we as human beings have found ourselves mobilized, inspired, moved, and ennobled by the stands that other people have taken. In fact, it is the willingness of others who have gone before us to take and hold their stand that has shaped the very world into which we were born. The authors of the Declaration of Independence were a stand for the freedom and political rights of every man. Abraham Lincoln was a stand for the unity of the nation and the freedom of slaves. Martin Luther King Jr. was a stand for civil rights and the dignity of all Americans. Mother Teresa was a stand for tending to the sick and the poor. In each case, we find people who made and held their stands in the face of political resistance, personal danger, and public disapproval. To be a stand is not about playing it safe. It is about staking your identity and your very future on what you believe. You step into authentic power when you embody your stand.

The names I cite above are clearly high-profile examples, but the phenomenon is universal. Each and every one of us has the opportunity to make and be our own unique stand in the world. The fact that we are not players on the world stage does not diminish the challenge and power of the act. Every day, school-teachers live out their stand for the future of our children. Every day, doctors and nurses live out their stand for the health and dignity of people. Every day, clergy, ministers, gurus, and shamans embody their stand for the power of spirit by guiding those who seek a deeper connection to the mysteries of life. We will never know the identities of all these people, yet we know them intimately by who and what they are for the rest of us, by their dedication, by their stand.

To be a stand means finding that cause, concern, or need in the world that you are passionate about attending to, and staking your life on your capacity to make a difference. It is the central move that you make in becoming an adult and taking your place in the world. Unfortunately, our society today is intensely focused on adolescent culture: the cult of me, mine, and now. It caters to the individual ego and keeps us from the deeper experience of a meaningful life. In declaring your stand, you step out of the small life that is centered on "me" and into a larger life that is centered on the world and your place in it.

The historical figures listed above demonstrate the galvanizing power that being a stand can have on both an individual and the world. Each of the people I mentioned above was both shaped by and in turn shaped the world with his or her stand. That's why they are powerful historical figures. But none of them simply woke up one day and, out of the blue, said, "I see it now. I will be a stand for freedom and dignity!"

It isn't that simple. We all arrive at our stand over time. It is an organic, evolving process. It entails using our awareness while allowing our interactions with the world to shape our concerns. We then learn to articulate those concerns and choose to act on them. Now you can begin to see how the components we have worked on so far fall into place.

You must hold yourself as able and be willing to act on your stand. Your stand has no power if you aren't willing to be account-able for and committed to it. In the process of articulating and embodying your stand, you will have ongoing opportunities to build and rebuild trust and to be honest with people. In the end, you are the one who will know if your thoughts, words, and actions are in integrity with your stand. When this alignment occurs, you will find your life dramatically more fulfilling and satisfying. Let's look at how the process unfolds.

Martin Luther King Jr. wasn't born caring about civil rights and dignity. He was shaped by his family and its tradition in the minis-try. He was shaped by the historical moment into which he was born and the people who influenced his learning and growth, the historical discourse of the country, and the events of his time. All of these factors influenced him to articulate his concern for civil rights and human dignity. As part of this process, there came a moment when he stood up and declared this as his stand.

What I want you to see is that events shaped each of these his-torical figures, just as events shape all of us. A stand does not just arrive out of nowhere, nor is it constructed out of nothing. Instead, it is forged out of the cares and concerns that arise from your inter-actions with the world, and the courage and resolve that arise within you.

This is the process by which each of us articulates and declares his or her unique way of being human in this world. The stand that you are is determined by how the world has shaped you, by what it has given you, and by what you rise up and claim for yourself. *Some is given; some you must claim!*

Over my years of work, I have observed many people who don't know what they stand for and who never declare themselves to the world. These are people who are easily tossed by the waves of life. They are constantly overwhelmed, confused, left behind, and wast-ing their lives "getting ready." They are ruled by the emotions of the moment and are always swayed by the latest and greatest new fashion, fad, or trend. Their lives tend to focus on the small me: my wants, my feelings, my fun, my freedom. They miss the bigger opportunity to take their place and truly be in the world. This is not the way to realize the potential and power that each of us has been given, and is clearly not the way to a new you.

I am a stand for the full and free expression of the human spirit, and that stand is the foundation for the work that we do at the Human Potential Project. Our ongoing commitment is to generate dignity, power, spirit, gratitude, and joy in the people that we work with. That means that we will do whatever is necessary to guide you in rising up and claiming your next level of expression. I have given you the building blocks you need. Now it's time to help you articulate who you are and what you stand for in this world. It is time to complete your transformation.

As I said above, a stand is a deep, life-shaping declaration. It is the declaration that announces to the world what you care about and what you dedicate your life to. A stand is different from a commitment, which is time- and measurement-bound. Here is an example. I am a stand for the ongoing education and development of my daughter. This stand will shape my actions for my entire life. In accordance with this stand, I will make a series of commitments. These commitments will change as my daughter grows and her needs change, but my stand for her will be permanent and fixed.

A stand is a deep and profound move that arises from my desire to make a difference in the world. It serves as a touchstone in my life. It is the means by which I resolve such questions as "What do I do now?" that leave others baffled. For example, if you are clear that you are a stand for the safety and well-being of children, then you will most likely focus your career in this area. You may be a teacher or school administrator, or a family counselor, or you might work with a foundation or in law enforcement, specializing in this area. At home, you will work to ensure that your family life is consistent with your stand. You will speak up when you see something occurring in your community that is not consistent with your stand.

A stand is much more than a career choice. With your stand as a guide, you won't get caught up in second-guessing yourself or envying people who have made and since lost millions in the stock market. You will not spend time in "if only" conversations with yourself when the world changes around you. Instead, firm in your stand and flexible with your actions, you will look to see how you can best reconfigure yourself to take effective action to attend to the safety of children. Your stand serves as the foundation on which you construct the rest of your life. Declaring your stand is also the most powerful example of the generative power of language. In declaring your stand you are in that moment creating yourself.

Without such a foundation, life tends to become meaningless. Here is why: Your stand provides your life with a purpose. Without purpose, it's difficult to find meaning in anything. As human beings we invent and assign meaning to events and occurrences. *Meaning exists only in relation to purpose.*

If my purpose in life were to terrorize the United States, then a car bomb exploding in the capital would mean success for me. If my purpose in life is to protect the nation from terrorists, then that same car bomb would mean failure. There is no "inherent or absolute" meaning to the car bomb; it changes depending upon my purpose. Most people cannot see the causal relationship between a lack of purpose and a lack of meaning. What we can see is that life without meaning is the source of most of the emotional and psychological suffering in our society. You need to have a higher purpose, a stand, in order to give meaning to your actions and their consequences. If you have no deeper purpose, no stand, then it is easy to fall into mindless consuming and other indulgences that are the source of many of our personal and national breakdowns.

As I hope you are beginning to see, to be clear about your stand in life and to be willing to declare yourself to the world are not trivial matters. Making this declaration is a conscious process of choice that leads to what we call embodiment, which is the foundation upon which you design your life. You declare your stand and dedicate your life to embodying or being that stand.

From that point forward, you use your stand as your "center," as you make the decisions that shape your future. Being a stand enables you to be a proactive designer of life, as opposed to a reactive player in a game that you don't understand. You close off the nagging doubts and questions that plague most people throughout their lives. Being a stand is, in fact, a source of freedom. When you make this declaration, you free yourself from having to wonder continually what you are doing, where you are going, and what the purpose of your life is.

At the same time, I want to be clear that being a stand is not a permanent and rigid state, nor is it about becoming obsessed with one narrow aspect of life. This too leads to suffering. If I am a stand for the development of technology that enables people to interact around the world, this doesn't mean that I spend my entire life devoted to this work at the expense of my family. It means that this is the deep foundation upon which my life is built. I can be this stand and also be a responsible parent, a bike racer, a spiritual practitioner, or a jazz musician. These are all aspects of a rich, expansive life. My stand forms the sun around which all of these other planets can smoothly orbit.

The prospect of actually being a stand in life can leave many people overwhelmed. The common statement, "I don't know what it is I care about," is usually inaccurate. More likely, it's the case that, "I have never clearly articulated what it is I care about and have fallen into the habit of simply reacting to the world." Sadly, most people have never examined their lives and are uncertain of how to go about articulating what it is they really care about. Many people are shaken by what they perceive as the seemingly infinite number of choices for a stand. To allay this fear I will offer you a way of seeing the world that will make it a bit simpler.

When we look at the world, we see that one of the conditions of being human is that we all share a finite set of concerns. It is, in fact, these shared concerns that make us human. Here is a good inventory of human concerns.

- Education—learning to be effective in my world
- Career—the part of my life in which I develop competence and in which my public identity is at stake in addressing a concern in the world
- Work—what I do in exchange for money (this may or may not be connected to career)
- Money—generating resources for myself
- Family—children
- Aging parents
- Intimacy—marriage and relationships
- Technology—the tools we use for crafting and moving in our world
- Play and recreation
- Social networks—friends and communities of interest
- Body—physical well-being
- Spirituality—my connection to the sacred
- The world—future generations, historical trends
- Mood—relationship to the future
- Identity and dignity

These concerns transcend cultures and historical epochs, and while the list is fairly wide in range, it is not infinite.

Read over this list and see which concerns call to you and seem relevant. Once you have identified what you deem to be core concerns, you can calmly and clearly craft a stand and thus bring a higher order of coherence to the various activities of your life. Accomplishing this will allow you to enjoy living in integrity.

Now that you have a sense of what a stand is and the power it can have in your life, and you've identified your core concerns, we will turn our attention to bringing some clarity to your stand.

To help you in this task, I am going to ask you a series of questions. The questions are intended to produce contemplation, but I don't want you to get lost in it. Answer them authentically; don't just tell me what you think I want to hear. Consider each question deeply. It may take you a few sessions to work through all of the questions. That's fine: After all, we're pouring the foundation for your future. Another hour or day is well worth the investment.

As you proceed, remember that each of us takes many stands in our lives. We have a stand on our finances, our families, and our health. While none of us is limited to just one stand, we each have one that takes precedence over the others. This is the one that matters most to us and is the core of who we are, and it is this stand to which I want to bring clarity and focus.

Also remember that there is no one right way to declare your stand. Some people embrace the process joyfully, regarding it as a tremendous opportunity and gift. For others, being asked to declare a stand produces panic, resignation, and even shame. For the first time in their lives, they may recognize their lack of a stand and worry that they won't be able to identify their passionate concern. While unsettling in the moment, this breakdown can lead to possibility in the long run. Turmoil arouses reflection and creates the means by which you can change the course of your life. This is my intention in offering the process to you.

ASSIGNMENT #12

ONE SECTION

TIME TO COMPLETE: IT'S UP TO YOU—A FEW
HOURS OR MORE

That's enough preamble. Let's get to work on your last assignment. As you should by now expect, I will ask that you write down the answers to these questions and be sure to save them. As most of you have been using your computers to do this, it ought to be simple.

1. What people, events, and historical trends have been instrumental in shaping who you are? Be specific here: Articulate names and occurrences, and explain how they have shaped you.

2. What do you see about how these influencing forces have shaped your interests and passions in life?

3. Which of the list of concerns that were provided earlier do you find the most affinity with? What do you care about deeply? To what aspects of life do you feel called upon to attend most consistently? Note: This is a moment to be wary of your inner cynic. Your truth is available to you. If what immediately comes to mind is something like "fishing, golfing, Manolo Blahniks," or the like, let yourself settle in more deeply and invite the cynic in you to give it a rest. This process is vital to your future, and you are up to something more profound than those trivial things.

4. Take a few moments and reflect on your life. Going as far back as you can, what do you see about the ways you have chosen to spend your time? What do these choices suggest that you care about?

5. What actions have you taken that demonstrate what it is you care about?

6. This question calls for a bit of imagination and visualization. Imagine yourself looking back through time at your own ancestors. You can easily see your parents, and most likely your grandparents. If you don't know your parents or grandparents, use your imagination and this moment to feel your connection to your own history. Look back further than those two generations. Imagine that you can look back through all the generations. Think of the sacrifices each generation made that enabled the next one to step up and take its place. Think of the stands your ancestors were, that now live as you. What did they stand for that you have inherited?

7. If they could speak to you, what would they say to you about the way you have lived your life?

8. Would they be proud of what you have made of your opportunities? Why do you say that?

9. Would they consider that their work and effort were well worth what you have made of it?

10. Delve deep into the core of your being and ask yourself what you are passionate about today.

11. In what aspect of life do you feel pulled to make a difference?

12. Project yourself into the future and consider your legacy, the story that people will tell about you when you are gone. What would you like to be said about the contribution you made to the world you left behind?

13. A stand is a first-person, present-tense declaration: "I am a stand for _____." Using that exact beginning, craft a version of a stand for yourself. To be most powerful, it should be brief and confined to one sentence. If your first cut produces something like, "I am a stand for kindness to all people," note that this is too vague and will not have power when you speak it. Focus this concern more sharply. "I am a stand for _____."

14. Declare your stand out loud to yourself. Does it sound genuine, authentic, embodied? Do you feel awkward when you say it?

15. Make any shifts in the wording of your stand that you think will make it more powerful, and then repeat it to yourself until you can make the declaration in a mood of genuine ownership. Practice it a number of times in the mirror and stay with it until you can look at yourself while declaring your stand and be proud of who you have become. Work through being embarrassed and stay with it until you get to embodiment, until you are not just saying your stand but being your stand. You can go to the Web site and receive some additional coaching on how to shape your somatic being to become more powerful and effective.

16. Crafting your stand is just the first step; now comes the real work. To declare your stand is to put yourself into a new game upon which you stake your identity and your integrity. Your job now is to examine your life and find the areas in which your priorities, commitments, and actions are inconsistent with your stand. You will want to spend time with this question. Look at all the aspects of your life: your work life, your personal life, your family life, your spiritual life, and so on. Where do you need to make changes in order to have your commitments and actions line up with your stand?

17. Write out the changes that you will need to make, and commit to how long it will take to complete these changes. Try to complete them within 30 days, or at least have them well under way. Your inner cynic will show up and try to talk you into taking your time or forgetting about some or all of them. Don't fall for it. Hold yourself to a rigorous timeline and get the changes made.

You now have a plan for bringing yourself into integrity with your new stand. Congratulations; you have completed the process.

If you have been working with a partner or team, you will want to share your process of discovery and declaration with them.

Don't be embarrassed by the occasional awkwardness that may arise. This is new territory, and you are all still beginners. If you have partners, share your timeline for life changes with them and enlist them to work with you to be sure that you stay on track with these deadlines. You can treat your partner or partners as customers for your promise to make these changes, and give them progress reports on how you are doing. You can, of course, also serve as the customer for their work on changing their lives. This process of change will unfold over time, but stay alert to the forces of inertia that will work to slow you down. Stay true and stand tall as the new you!

And now we have arrived at the end of our journey together. The transformation has been a success! You have completed the work of crafting a new version of you and are ready to step into a new future. As you move into the world having earned your place, you will discover that you have changed in more ways than you realized. As a person who moves through life dedicated to living, being, and embodying a new stand in life, you will find that the world now looks different to you. Your default behaviors won't satisfy you anymore, and you will find yourself stepping up into a higher order of action. Over time, you will find that the world will test you with a host of challenges. Don't worry. At each and every turn, *you know what to do.*

Everything moves from center, and that is the place to start. From center you can best access your awareness, and as you now know, greater awareness affords you a greater field of choice. You are infinitely able, so your ongoing issue will be your willingness. Are you willing to face the challenges and live your stand?

You are the only one who is accountable for your actions, and we will measure your commitment by your results, nothing more, nothing less. The new you lives in a world of possibility and action. You will be called upon to build and rebuild trust as you reconfigure yourself and your world. Honesty will be a vital tool in the process, and you now know the distinctions and practices of truth, so use them wisely.

Assembled into a new unity, you have a new standard for assessing your integrity. The you that looks back from the mirror knows when you are in or out of integrity. Look deeply into the eyes you see in the mirror and be true to yourself. Sometimes you will rise to the occasion of the trials that life throws at you and sometimes you will not. That is what it is to be human. Each experience will provide you with the opportunity to renew and strengthen your stand and validate your integrity. Every beat of your heart opens a new world of possibilities. This is where you will find your new future.

Congratulations—you have joined the small but growing number of people who are willing to be a powerful stand in life. This is the global collective of learners who are quietly assuming accountability for the future of our world. Living your life as the new you is the means by which you can and will build authentic power, lasting dignity, continued satisfaction, and, in the end, the peacefulness that comes from having contributed to the next generation by living your life well.

I want to acknowledge you for all of the work that you put into this process. I know that it isn't easy to face down your internal cynic, contend with the enemies of learning, and engage in authentic learning in a world that seems intent on distracting you and dissuading you from your mission. For that patience and perseverance, you have my admiration and respect. For granting me the trust to take you through the process, you have my heartfelt thanks.

OPTIONAL COMPLETION ASSIGNMENT

Here is a last little bit of work for you to do to tidy up the loose ends. With each of the assignments you have been given, I have asked that you write down your answers and save them. This is what we have been saving them for. Go back now and read through the answers to the various assignments and craft a simple narrative about what you see you have learned. How did your transformation unfold? How have you reshaped yourself, and what new possibilities do you now see that you didn't see when we started? Answer the simple question: Who is the new you, and how is the new you different from the original model?

Use this narrative as a means to acknowledge the progress that you have made. Share it with your partners if you are working with any, and if you are so inclined, send it to me at CDM@human potentialproject.com, because the HP2 team and I are always interested in seeing how we impact people's lives.

Again, thank you for your trust, and congratulations—a new world is waiting!

———————

ACKNOWLEDGMENTS

A project of this sort is never a simple undertaking, nor does it all originate from a single source. I have been building the Human Potential Project's body of work for some 25 years, and I am clear that it is still very much a work in progress. Over the years I have spent time studying with a variety of teachers, done research on my own, collaborated with others, and developed material from scratch. This is my opportunity to express my appreciation for the contributions my teachers have made to me, for the commitment and loyalty that my team has demonstrated, and for the thousands we have been privileged to touch over the years. For me the easiest way to do this is chronologically.

I got my inspiration to explore this new world of human potential from George Leonard and his book *The Ultimate Athlete*. George later became a teacher and coach, and he has spent time working with our staff. His work on mastery is reflected in our work and the material you will read on learning. Bill Maynard of the Effectiveness Institute convinced me that I could do this on my own and encouraged and eventually insisted that I do so.

Hirata Sensei was my aikido teacher and introduced me to the principles and practices of aikido, which remain fundamental to our somatic approach to teaching and learning. Will Schutz introduced me to some of the initial concepts that eventually became our Universal Performance Principles. He too spent time working with and in many cases shaking up our trainer body. Dr. Fernando

Flores's work on language and action played a pivotal role in the development of everything that we do. I spent a number of years learning from and eventually collaborating with Fernando, and his original work is deeply woven into everything that we do and certainly into this book. Julio Ollia and the Newfield group took the work on language and action to a deeper level and refined a body of work on learning and coaching. Dr. Richard Heckler and I shaped a paper on practices for centering that HP2 still uses. The seeds that were planted by these teachers and partners have grown into, are contained in, and were shaped into what you are about to read.

Over the years I have had the privilege of calling some extraordinary people teammates. The list is now too long to put into print, so I will say a heartfelt thanks to all of them in general and point to a cadre of core contributors. There is a picture on my desk of the original crew, which consisted of myself, Larry Burback, Bud Cooke, Joel Levey, Horst Abraham, and Jim Channon. This team crafted the original vision for and version of our work. The next wave included Jac Cirie and Mike Blondell, and I hired Dr. Richard Heckler to work with us on our Special Forces project. Jac became a big brother to me and was instrumental in helping the company through its first big expansion. Jac and Mike both left the world suddenly and tragically. Their commitment to a life of freedom remains as their legacy. Tom Lutes, Phil Bryson, and their On the Edge gang were energetic partners through our wild growth years and taught us all what partnership was about. Tom continues to provide these ongoing lessons. Maggie Weiss, Kim Loop, and Susan Smallidge helped me take the company through some very rough times, and we made it through a few rough times of our own. Our trainer body and coaching group have seen a host of people come and graduate on to other things. Through it all a strong cadre has both emerged and remained. Richard McDonald, Dan Haygeman, Juan Mobili, Susana Mantis, Todd Demorest, and Harry Sloofman have all been in our orbit for 20 years. They are held together by the example, energy, and ongoing commitment of Larry Burback and Kim Loop. In their own and very different ways each has helped hold the center of the company together through both the toughest and smoothest of times. Larry and I started playing rugby together at the University of Washington, and although people often liken us to the odd couple, he has been a brother in nearly every sense of the word. As a final tribute to the tribe, I want to point to Andy Ackemann. Andy started as a client and then became a teammate and team leader. Like Jac and Mike, he passed too soon but his spirit is with us.

I have also been the beneficiary of some good advice and counsel at the board level from the likes of Mike Wick, Jim Jensen, Tom Armstrong, Dave Ederer, Bob Mayes, and the late Dan Ward.

Today I like to tell myself that I have learned, via some at times very rough experience, what it really takes to build an enterprise from the ground up. While this won't be news, one of the key elements is a strong leadership and management team. In the moment I am clear that I have been blessed with the most competent and committed management team I ever imagined. Sue Kresovich, Peter Yaholkovsky, Sue Staker, and Joel Kimmel have enabled HP2 to flourish while at the same time preparing the firm for the next leap. Vibhuti Jha has opened new worlds for us as we look to expand internationally. While he is not an official member of the team, George Kresovich has been there with us through it all. To each and every one a sincere thanks.

Finally, there is Charles Koppelman and David Fritz at CAK Entertainment, and Steve Murphy, Shannon Welch, and the good people at Rodale. They understood the vision of what was possible and how we could bring something new to the world. Without their trust, you would not be reading any of this.

So to all of them go my thanks, and to all of you, it's time to get to work. There is a new future waiting for you.

INDEX

Boldface page references indicate illustrations.

ABOUT THE AUTHOR

Chris Majer is the Founder and Chief Executive Officer of The Human Potential Project. He began his work and career as an entrepreneur and competitive rugby player. After earning a master's degree in public administration from the University of Washington, he worked as a political consultant for a number of years. In 1981, he founded the first iteration of HP2. Their original work was focused on athletes, and their success with individuals and teams caught the attention of the military. The company then designed and delivered a series of groundbreaking programs to the U.S. Army, and with that solid foundation, they took the work to the corporate world, where they were soon generating remarkable results. Under Mr. Majer's leadership, the firm grew from a start-up to a company of more than 80 professionals working globally. Mr. Majer was the principal architect of organizational transformation projects for such corporate clients as AT&T, Cargill, Microsoft, Intel, EDS, Amgen, Capital One, and Allianz Life. Over the years, he has worked with a number of nationally recognized teachers, including George Leonard, Will Schutz, and Dr. Fernando Flores. In addition, he was an aikido student for a number of years. All of these influences have shaped his work. He lives in the state of Washington, which serves as the base for his travels and adventures.